THE LAUREL POETRY SERIES *is unique in the growing range of fine, inexpensive paperbound books. Each volume contains the works of a single poet, along with an original introduction, a chronology of the poet's career, a bibliography and notes on the poetry.*

RUTHVEN TODD, *born in Edinburgh and now a permanent resident of Martha's Vineyard, has farmed, taught, painted, edited and written. He has published three novels, several volumes of poetry (a volume of "Selected Poems" is now in preparation), a book of essays, several children's books, and books on painters and illustrators, including William Blake, which Todd edited.*

RICHARD WILBUR, *the General Editor, has won the Pulitzer Prize, the National Book Award, and the Millay Prize, all three in 1957 for his book of poems, "Things of This World." He has published several other volumes of poetry, as well as a translation of Molière's "The Misanthrope." Mr. Wilbur has held a Guggenheim and a Prix de Rome Fellowship, and is a member of the National Institute of Arts and Letters He is now Professor of English at Wesleyan University, and has taught at Harvard and Wellesley.*

OTHER VOLUMES AVAILABLE IN THE LAUREL POETRY SERIES:

The Laurel Poetry Series

General Editor, Richard Wilbur

Blake

Selected poetry, with
an introduction and notes
by Ruthven Todd

Published by
DELL PUBLISHING CO., INC.
750 Third Avenue
New York 17, N.Y.

Laurel ® TM 674623, Dell Publishing Co., Inc.

Typography by Alvin Eisenman

Produced by Western Printing and Lithographing Company

Cover drawing by Richard Powers

First printing: September, 1960
Second printing: November, 1963
Third printing: November, 1964
Fourth printing: March, 1966
Fifth printing: September, 1967
Sixth printing: April, 1969
Seventh printing: April, 1970
Eighth printing: September, 1971

Printed in U.S.A.

Contents

Introduction

The world into which William Blake was born in 1757 was a very different world from that which we know today. This may seem a truism, but it is one which has to be restated time and again. If we forget it we tend to judge the past by standards which that past did not know and would not recognize. We cannot understand that past, for instance, if we forget that Blake and his contemporaries were ruled in their views of history and mythology by the necessity of accepting the date of the Creation as 4004 B.C., a date established in the seventeenth century by the ingenious Bishop James Ussher. Blake, although an original, was also in many ways a man of his own time—a time of experiment and turmoil.

Taking the whole of his output, paintings and engravings included, as a single body of work, one realizes quickly that Blake was a stubbornly single-minded man. His ambition was to create a vast synthesis, pictorial as well as poetic, into which he could fold everything, all history and all mythology, as well as his own personal beliefs. Sometimes, it seems, in reaching for the poetic expression for this vast personal mythology and philosophy, he went beyond the bounds of poetry. Large passages of the so-called Prophetic Books are fascinating reading indeed for those who have the time and the knowledge to study them carefully, and they cast a great deal of light upon the mind of the man who was William Blake. But, as is the trouble with all personal mythologies upon such a tremendous scale, there are many references which must remain forever obscure, and many stretches where there is just not enough poetry to carry the obscurity. These books are, of course, more literate than the "prophecies" of Richard Brothers and Joanna Southcott, but, at the same time, there is a good deal of those "prophets" in the method and form of expression; as much, in fact, as there is of James Macpherson with his *Ossian*, an influence which Blake admitted. Macpherson took as his starting point the fragments of an acknowledged, and verbally transmitted, mythology. Blake set out to create his own.

Having been born in the first year of Swendenborg's new era, when "a new heaven is begun, and . . . the Eternal Hell revives," Blake grew up in an atmosphere of visionary Christianity. So it was to be expected that he would draw largely upon Biblical mythology. But the Biblical figures which appear in the Prophetic Books (as I shall continue to call them for the sake of convenience) are not the figures which actually appear in the Bible itself. Jesus is not Jesus of Nazareth but a rebel angel, the embodiment of all that is desirable in religion and the destroyer of evil laws. Abraham, Heber, Shem and Noah are Druids, for Blake believed that "All things Begin & End in Albion's Ancient Druid Rocky Shore." In believing this, Blake goes no farther than Milton, who wrote: "Writers of good antiquity, and ablest judgement have bin perswaded that ev'n the school of *Pythagoras* and the *Persian* wisdom took beginning from the old Philosophy of this Iland." Jerusalem is not a city in Palestine, but a personalized symbol. In this too, Blake was caught up in the spirit of his times. Sir Isaac Newton had considered his researches on the original plan of the Temple in Jerusalem as infinitely more valuable than his scientific work, and Richard Brothers, the self-styled "Nephew of the Almighty," and founder of the British Israelites, had ambitions of rebuilding the city in accordance with a plan revealed to him by his Almighty relative. In the "prophecies" of Joanna Southcott, too, Jerusalem is not a place but a personality. So Blake mingled his "Biblical" figures with others drawn from a multitude of sources.

On the other hand, unlike his contemporaries, Blake drew little upon classical mythology. In the eighteenth century the use of the classical myths had become little more than ornamental, an embroidery upon the ideas of the poet, and Blake could not rest content with such a façade. "Let it here be Noted," he wrote, "that the Greek Fables originated in Spiritual Mystery & Real Visions, which are lost & clouded in Fable & allegory, while the Hebrew Bible & the Greek Gospel are Genuine, Preserv'd by the Saviour's Mercy. The Nature of my Work is Visionary or Imaginative; it is an endeavour to Restore what the Ancients call'd the Golden Age. This world of Imagination is Infinite & Eternal, whereas the world of Generation, or Vegetation, is Finite & Temporal. There exist in that Eternal World the Permanent Realities of Every Thing we see reflected in this Vegetable Glass of Nature." He could not accept a convention in which "Bloated Gods, Mercury, Juno, Venus, & the rattle traps of Mythology & the lumber of an awkward French Palace are thrown together around Clumsy & Ricketty Princes & Princesses higgledy piggledy." The creatures of his own mythology may often be obscure but they are never merely decorative.

The remarkable thing is that, from such a complexity of symbols and such an ambitious and elaborate structure, so much poetry of such high quality should remain.

Only two of Blake's books of poems, *Poetical Sketches*, 1783, and *The French Revolution*, 1791, were produced by conventional printing methods. It is a fairly reasonable supposition that *Poetical Sketches* was printed by the order of Blake's admirers, the Rev. Anthony Stephen Matthews, pastor of Percy Chapel in London, and John Flaxman, the sculptor. All the poems in the book were written before the poet had reached the age of twenty-one, and a contemporary states that "How sweet I roam'd" was written before Blake's fourteenth year. The rather patronizing Advertisement, probably written by Matthews, states, "The following Sketches were the production of untutored youth, commenced in his twelfth, and occasionally resumed by the author till his twentieth year; since which time, his talents having been wholly directed to the attainment of excellence in his profession, he has been deprived of the leisure requisite to such a revisal of these sheets, as might have rendered them less unfit to meet the public eye. Conscious of the irregularities and defects to be found in almost every page, his friends have still believed that they possessed a poetical originality, which merited some respite from oblivion. These their opinions remain, however, to be now reproved or confirmed by a less partial public."

(The tone of this preface may have had something to do with Blake's decision to become his own publisher, if one can call him that. In his early satire, "An Island in the Moon," his ideas were grandiose: "I would have all the writing Engraved instead of Printed, & at every other leaf a high finish'd print—all in three Volumes folio—& sell them a hundred pounds apiece. They would print off two thousand." This was a dream which he never succeeded in accomplishing. However, the method which he worked out was one which gave him such personal satisfaction that, once he had perfected it, he never, with the exception of *The French Revolution* which exists only in a unique set of page proofs, thought of using the conventional methods of production again.)

These early poems show a strange collection of influences. On the one hand there are the Elizabethans, notably Spenser and Shakespeare, and the smattering of eighteenth-century poets such as Watts, Thomson, Chatterton, Collins and the rest. On the other, and rather stranger side, but more pertinent to the development of Blake, are the peculiarities of *Ossian,* and the ornateness of the prose of James Hervey, author of *Meditations and Contemplations* (a book from which, incidentally, Blake also drew the material for one of his watercolors). When

T. S. Eliot drew attention to the young Blake's "immense power of assimilation," he was right, but failed to point out that, although these early poems do show a great deal of the influence of the eighteenth century in the use of conventional "poeticized" epithets, Blake was not really interested in the perfecting of their use or in the strict diction of his verse. He had something to say and he said it as well as he could, even if it did require the wrenching around of the Spenserian stanza and the use of half-rhymes. *Poetical Sketches* are the juvenilia of a poet who is working his way toward the perfecting of the tools which will enable him to undertake a vaster and more elaborate construction.

Once Blake had reached maturity with the issuing of the *Songs of Innocence*, his poetry, although it exists in its own right, became for him merely a part of a whole. The imagery in most of the poems did not *need* to be intensely visual. The visual was to be carried by the designs with which, in his own methods, he surrounded each poem. Blake intended his text and his illuminations to form one indivisible whole. He could not see the poems as existing apart from the decorations. This intention is shown most obviously in certain passages of his *Milton* and *Jerusalem* where a passage of text appears in reverse. The reason for this is that it was meant to be read, not from the external world, but from the internal one: "Mental things are alone Real. . . ." He did not imagine the poems as existing apart from these designs.

However, despite this intention on the part of the poet, the poems are often much more vivid than the designs which accompany them. The miniature parade of boys and girls which goes with "Holy Thursday" adds little to the poetry:

> 'Twas on a Holy Thursday, their innocent faces clean
> The children walking two & two, in red & blue & green,

Grey-headed beadles walk'd before, with wands as
white as snow,
Till into the high dome of Paul's they like Thames'
waters flow.

On the other hand, the cupped flower within which a mother holds a child being blessed by a butterfly-winged angel, adds immeasurably to one's appreciation of "Infant Joy":

"I have no name:
I am but two days old."
What shall I call thee?
"I happy am,
Joy is my name."
Sweet joy befall thee!

This poem, which we today accept in all its simplicity, is a striking example of Blake's ability to make use of whatever he found. Directly, of course, it owes something to Isaac Watts' *Divine Songs Attempted in Easy Language*, as well as to the Elizabethans, but it, despite the inversion of "I happy am," and the rest of the *Songs of Innocence*, marks a clean break with the fashionable "poetical" language of the eighteenth century which Blake had used in *Poetical Sketches*, a book for the printing of which he had no responsibility.

By the time he was ready to print *Songs of Experience*, Blake had assimilated and mixed with his simplicity even more of the strange influence of *Ossian* and, it seems probable, of the Druidical influence of Thomas Gray. In 1785, he had exhibited at the Royal Academy a watercolor from Gray, "The Bard" (and was to show a tempera of the same subject in his 1809 exhibition); he further prepared an elaborate illustrated folio of designs surrounding Gray's *Poems* which was not printed in his lifetime. The *Songs*, however, have digested their influences so well that by now it could be no other than Blake himself speaking If one were to dissect "The Tyger," for instance, one might be able to pinpoint fragmentary echoes, but as a whole it is Blake alone. Incidentally, the spelling of the word "tiger" with a "y" instead of an "i" seems to be a visual expression; the "y" exaggerates the suggestion of a trigger or a coiled spring pertinent to the tense and awful tyger.

By this time, too, there is a growing sense of abstraction and of the personification of ideas, as in "The Human Abstract":

> Pity would be no more
> If we did not make somebody Poor;
> And Mercy no more could be
> If all were as happy as we.
>
> And mutual fear brings peace,
> Till the selfish loves increase:
> Then Cruelty knits a snare,
> And spreads his baits with care.

This growth away from the concrete particulars of the songs of childhood and early manhood becomes increasingly evident in all of Blake's subsequent work. The lyric as a form of expression was no longer sufficient for Blake, although he could, when he desired, use it with superb effect as in the famous lines from "Milton":

> And did those feet in ancient time
> Walk upon England's mountains green?
> And was the holy Lamb of God
> On England's pleasant pastures seen?
>
> And did the Countenance Divine
> Shine forth upon our clouded hills?
> And was Jerusalem builded here
> Among these dark Satanic Mills?
>
> Bring me my Bow of burning gold:
> Bring me my Arrows of Desire:
> Bring me my Spear: O clouds unfold!
> Bring me my Chariot of fire.

I will not cease from Mental Fight,
Nor shall my Sword sleep in my hand
Till we have built Jerusalem
In England's green & pleasant Land.

These stanzas were presumably written about 1804, and after that the lyrical mode of expression seems to languish, except about 1818 in the fine "Epilogue" to *The Gates of Paradise*:

Truly, My Satan, thou art but a Dunce,
And dost not know the Garment from the Man.
Every Harlot was a Virgin once,
Nor can'st thou ever change Kate into Nan.

Tho' thou art Worship'd by the Names Divine
Of Jesus & Jehovah, thou art still
The Son of Morn in Weary Night's decline,
The lost Traveller's Dream under the Hill.

In all his lyrics after the early *Poetical Sketches*, Blake seems to have been in search of a directness which his century ignored. "How wide the Gulf & Unpassable between Simplicity and Insipidity," he wrote, and he never made the error of confusing one with the other. Watts' verses are only too often insipid, as if the effort of writing hymns for children also meant that they had to be wrapped in sugar, like taffy-apples. Blake, on the other hand, achieves simplicity which is never saccharine.

Although *The Marriage of Heaven and Hell* can hardly be described as a "poem" in the commonly accepted sense of the word, I have included it here because it contains so much that is vitally pertinent to Blake's thought and development. If it is not a "poem," furthermore, it is difficult to see what else it is: the prose as well as the thought have grown a long way from "An Island in the Moon." It is taut and expressive and wastes nothing. If one considers the Bible as poetry, then the "Proverbs of Hell" are also poetry. They may be Blake's contradictions and corrections of John Caspar Lavater's

Aphorisms on Man, for which he had engraved a plate after his friend Henry Fuseli in 1788, and which he had annotated in his own copy, but they are far more than that. If their primary intention seems to be to shock the reader into thought, they are also the basic tenets of Blake's belief.

All his life Blake believed in the eternal and necessary coexistence of Good and Evil:

> Without Contraries is no progression. Attraction and Repulsion, Reason and Energy, Love and Hate, are necessary to Human existence.
>
> From these contraries spring what the religious call Good & Evil. Good is the passive that obeys Reason. Evil is the active springing from Energy.
>
> Good is Heaven. Evil is Hell.

But for Blake, the usual terms of Good and Evil had become reversed. The angel which would trammel man in the bonds of religion and reason was evil, while the devil which released him from such bonds was good:

> All Bibles or sacred codes have been the causes of the following Errors:
>
> 1. That Man has two real existing principles: Viz: a Body & a Soul.
> 2. That Energy, call'd Evil, is alone from the Body; and that Reason, call'd Good, is alone from the Soul.
> 3. That God will torment Man in Eternity for following his Energies.
>
> But the following Contraries to these are True:
>
> 1. Man has no Body distinct from his Soul; for that call'd Body is a portion of Soul discern'd by the five Senses, the chief inlets of Soul in this age.
> 2. Energy is the only life, and is from the Body; and Reason is the bound or outward circumference of Energy.

3. Energy is Eternal Delight.

Blake's remark in *The Marriage of Heaven and Hell* about Milton is also applicable to himself: "The reason Milton wrote in fetters when he wrote of Angels & God, and at liberty when of Devils & Hell, is because he was a true Poet and of the Devil's party without knowing it." *The Marriage of Heaven and Hell,* devoted to its investigation into the various kinds of energy, is a plea for freedoms, and in particular for the freedom to recognize that the body is a part of the soul, and vice versa.

From this time on, Blake's long works are written in a free verse form, with a stronger cadence than that used in the more or less poetical prose of his youth. And now, too, they become peopled with all his symbolical figures who perform in an eternal and not a temporal world. Still, however, there are magnificent passages, such as the outburst in "America":

> The morning comes, the night decays, the watchmen leave their stations;
> The grave is burst, the spices shed, the linen wrapped up;
> The bones of death, the cov'ring clay, the sinews shrunk & dry'd
> Reviving shake, inspiring move, breathing, awakening,
> Spring like redeemed captives when their bonds & bars are burst.
> Let the slave grinding at the mill run out into the field,
> Let him look up into the heavens & laugh in the bright air;
> Let the inchained soul, shut up in darkness and in sighing,
> Whose face has never seen a smile in thirty weary years,
> Rise and look out; his chains are loose, his dungeon doors are open;

And let his wife and children return from the oppressor's scourge.

Now Blake is more concerned to be a teacher than to be a poet, although he is still involved in the making of beauty, as the magnificent colored copy of *Jerusalem*, reproduced by the Blake Trust and now at Yale, shows. It is hard to think of him in his latter years as a poet alone, for the mind always wanders to think of the illustrations to the Book of Job, and the drawings done in illustration of Dante.

Although it would be fair to place Blake among the greatest of Englishmen, it would not be correct to claim for him supreme greatness in any single aspect of the things which he attempted. His lyrical poems are often rough and pay little attention to the niceties of prosody, his didactic and symbolical works are too often formless and obscure, and even as an artist, although he may have been, as Fuseli claimed, "damned good to steal from," the ideas frequently outrun his powers of execution. Why then do we claim greatness for this comparative failure?

It is because in a world of little men, men like mice chewing away at their little corners, he stands out like a giant, like his own Albion. He was truly a "Mental Prince," and in all his ideas he says much that we today are only beginning to recognize as true. When W. H. Auden said that "The whole of Freud's teaching may be found in *The Marriage of Heaven and Hell,*" he may have been exaggerating, but the fact remains that Blake was, as a psychologist, far ahead of his times, and his longer works are source books which spark ideas in others. His thought may be unorganized and hard to disentangle, but the kernels of truth which it contains make the quest well worth while. As Blake himself said, "The ruins of Time build mansions in Eternity."

RUTHVEN TODD
November, 1959

BIBLIOGRAPHICAL NOTE

The early sources for Blake's life are reprinted in Arthur Symons, *William Blake* (1907). The first biography, Alexander Gilchrist, *Life of William Blake* (1863, 1880), was edited, with notes and a full bibliography, by Ruthven Todd for Everyman's Library (1942, 1945). The best modern book is Mona Wilson, *Life of William Blake* (1927, revised 1948), but Thomas Wright, *Life of William Blake* (1929), contains much not available elsewhere, as does Geoffrey Keynes, *Blake Studies* (1949).

There are many interpretations of Blake, but as those before 1944 are listed in the Everyman's bibliography, only a few later ones are mentioned here. These include J. Bronowski, *William Blake, a Man without a Mask* (1943, revised in Pelican Books, 1954), Mark Schorer, *William Blake, The Politics of Vision* (1946), Ruthven Todd, *Tracks in the Snow* (1946), Northrop Frye, *Fearful Symmetry* (1947, 1958), J. G. Davies, *The Theology of William Blake* (1948), Bernard Blackstone, *English Blake* (1949), David V. Erdman, *Blake, Prophet against Empire* (1954), George Wingfield Digby, *Symbol and Image in William Blake.* An important work is in preparation by Miss Kathleen Raine.

The definitive text is Keynes' edition of *The Complete Writings of William Blake with All the Variant Readings.* Here that text has been collated with the same editor's *Poetry and Prose of William Blake* (1927, 1948), for which acknowledgments are due to Sir Geoffrey Keynes, The Nonesuch Press and Random House.

As Blake intended his works to be seen as a whole, a few facsimiles which should be available in first-class libraries are listed. *The Marriage of Heaven and Hell* (1927), *The Book of Thel* (1928), *The Book of Urizen* (1929), *Visions of the Daughters of Albion* (1932), *Jerusalem* (colored, 1951), *Jerusalem* (black and white,

1952), *Songs of Innocence* (1954), *Songs of Innocence and of Experience* (1955). More on Blake's methods will be found in "The Techniques of William Blake's Illuminated Painting" (*sic*, for "Printing"), Ruthven Todd, *Print*, VI, 1 (1948).

Chronology

1757 November 28, born in London.

1768 Entered Pars' Drawing School in the Strand.

1772 August 4, apprenticed as engraver to James Basire.

1779 October 8, finished apprenticeship. Started engraving for booksellers.

1780 Involved in June riots.

1782 August 18, married Catherine Boucher.

1783 *Poetical Sketches* printed.

1784 Opened print shop in partnership with James Parker, 27 Broad Street. Wrote *An Island in the Moon.*

1787 February, death of brother Robert. Partnership dissolved. Moved to 28 Poland Street.

1788 *No Natural Religion* etc., booklets.

1789 *Thel; Songs of Innocence.*

1790 *The Marriage of Heaven and Hell.*

1791 *The French Revolution* printed.

1793 Moved to 13 Hercules Buildings, Lambeth. *Gates of Paradise.* Prospectus offered *Visions of the Daughters of Albion, America, Songs of Experience* etc.

1794 *Songs of Innocence and of Experience, Europe, Book of Urizen.*

1795 *Book of Los, Book of Ahania, Song of Los.*

1800 September 18, moved to Felpham.

1803 August 12, encounter with Schofield and Cock. Moved to 17 South Molton Street.

1804 January 12, tried at Chichester, acquitted. Started *Milton* and *Jerusalem.*

1808 Designs for Blair's *Grave* published. *Milton* finished.

1809 Blake's exhibition at 28 Broad Street.

1818 Worked on *Jerusalem*. Met John Linnell.

1819 Visionary Heads for John Varley.

1820 Colored copy of *Jerusalem* finished.

1821 Sold his print collection. Moved to 2 Fountain Court, Strand.

1825 *Illustrations of the Book of Job.*

1827 August 12, died.

from *Poetical Sketches*

To Spring

O thou with dewy locks, who lookest down*
Thro' the clear windows of the morning, turn
Thine angel eyes upon our western isle,
Which in full choir hails thy approach, O Spring!

The hills tell each other, and the list'ning
Vallies hear; all our longing eyes are turned
Up to thy bright pavillions: issue forth,
And let thy holy feet visit our clime.

Come o'er the eastern hills, and let our winds
Kiss thy perfumed garments; let us taste
Thy morn and evening breath; scatter thy pearls
Upon our love-sick land that mourns for thee.

O deck her forth with thy fair fingers; pour
Thy soft kisses on her bosom; and put
Thy golden crown upon her languish'd head,
Whose modest tresses were bound up for thee!

To Summer

O thou, who passest thro' our vallies in
Thy strength, curb thy fierce steeds, allay the heat
That flames from their large nostrils! thou, O Summer,
Oft pitched'st here thy golden tent, and oft
Beneath our oaks hast slept, while we beheld
With joy thy ruddy limbs and flourishing hair.

Beneath our thickest shades we oft have heard
Thy voice, when noon upon his fervid car

*Notes appear together beginning on p. 157.

Rode o'er the deep of heaven; beside our springs
Sit down, and in our mossy vallies, on
Some bank beside a river clear, throw thy
Silk draperies off, and rush into the stream:
Our vallies love the Summer in his pride.

Our bards are fam'd who strike the silver wire:
Our youth are bolder than the southern swains:
Our maidens fairer in the sprightly dance:
We lack not songs, nor instruments of joy,
Nor echoes sweet, nor waters clear as heaven,
Nor laurel wreaths against the sultry heat.

To Autumn

O Autumn, laden with fruit, and stained
With the blood of the grape, pass not, but sit
Beneath my shady roof; there thou may'st rest,
And tune thy jolly voice to my fresh pipe;
And all the daughters of the year shall dance!
Sing now the lusty song of fruits and flowers.

"The narrow bud opens her beauties to
The sun, and love runs in her thrilling veins;
Blossoms hang round the brows of morning, and
Flourish down the bright cheek of modest eve,
Till clust'ring Summer breaks forth into singing,
And feather'd clouds strew flowers round her head.

"The spirits of the air live on the smells
Of fruit; and joy, with pinions light, roves round
The gardens, or sits singing in the trees."
Thus sang the jolly Autumn as he sat;
Then rose, girded himself, and o'er the bleak
Hills fled from our sight; but left his golden load.

To Winter

O Winter! bar thine adamantine doors:
The north is thine; there hast thou built thy dark
Deep-founded habitation. Shake not thy roofs,
Nor bend thy pillars with thine iron car.

He hears me not, but o'er the yawning deep
Rides heavy; his storms are unchain'd, sheathed
In ribbed steel; I dare not lift mine eyes,
For he hath rear'd his sceptre o'er the world.

Lo! now the direful monster, whose skin clings
To his strong bones, strides o'er the groaning rocks:
He withers all in silence, and his hand
Unclothes the earth, and freezes up frail life.

He takes his seat upon the cliffs; the mariner
Cries in vain. Poor little wretch! that deal'st
With storms, till heaven smiles, and the monster
Is driv'n yelling to his caves beneath mount Hecla.

To the Evening Star

Thou fair-hair'd angel of the evening,
Now, whilst the sun rests on the mountains, light
Thy bright torch of love; thy radiant crown
Put on, and smile upon our evening bed!
Smile on our loves, and, while thou drawest the
Blue curtains of the sky, scatter thy silver dew
On every flower that shuts its sweet eyes
In timely sleep. Let thy west wind sleep on
The lake; speak silence with thy glimmering eyes,
And wash the dusk with silver. Soon, full soon,
Dost thou withdraw; then the wolf rages wide,
And the lion glares thro' the dun forest:

The fleeces of our flocks are cover'd with
Thy sacred dew: protect them with thine influence.

To Morning

O holy virgin! clad in purest white,
Unlock heav'n's golden gates, and issue forth;
Awake the dawn that sleeps in heaven; let light
Rise from the chambers of the east, and bring
The honied dew that cometh on waking day.
O radiant morning, salute the sun,
Rouz'd like a huntsman to the chace, and, with
Thy buskin'd feet, appear upon our hills.

Song

How sweet I roam'd from field to field,
  And tasted all the summer's pride,
'Til I the prince of love beheld,
  Who in the sunny beams did glide!

He shew'd me lilies for my hair,
  And blushing roses for my brow;
He led me through his gardens fair,
  Where all his golden pleasures grow.

With sweet May dews my wings were wet,
  And Phoebus fir'd my vocal rage;
He caught me in his silken net,
  And shut me in his golden cage.

He loves to sit and hear me sing,
  Then, laughing, sports and plays with me;
Then stretches out my golden wing,
  And mocks my loss of liberty.

Song

My silks and fine array,
  My smiles and languish'd air,
By love are driv'n away;
  And mournful lean Despair
Brings me yew to deck my grave:
Such end true lovers have.

His face is fair as heav'n,
  When springing buds unfold;
O why to him was't giv'n,
  Whose heart is wintry cold?
His breast is love's all worship'd tomb,
Where all love's pilgrims come.

Bring me an axe and spade,
  Bring me a winding sheet;
When I my grave have made,
  Let winds and tempests beat:
Then down I'll lie, as cold as clay.
True love doth pass away!

Song

Love and harmony combine,
And around our souls intwine,
While thy branches mix with mine,
And our roots together join.

Joys upon our branches sit,
Chirping loud, and singing sweet;
Like gentle streams beneath our feet
Innocence and virtue meet.

Thou the golden fruit dost bear,
I am clad in flowers fair;

Thy sweet boughs perfume the air,
And the turtle buildeth there.

There she sits and feeds her young,
Sweet I hear her mournful song;
And thy lovely leaves among,
There is love: I hear his tongue.

There his charming nest doth lay,
There he sleeps the night away;
There he sports along the day,
And doth among our branches play.

Song

I love the jocund dance,
  The softly-breathing song,
Where innocent eyes do glance,
  And where lisps the maiden's tongue.

I love the laughing vale,
  I love the echoing hill,
Where mirth does never fail,
  And the jolly swain laughs his fill.

I love the pleasant cot,
  I love the innocent bow'r,
Where white and brown is our lot,
  Or fruit in the mid-day hour.

I love the oaken seat,
  Beneath the oaken tree,
Where all the old villagers meet,
  And laugh our sports to see.

I love our neighbours all,
  But, Kitty, I better love thee;

And love them I ever shall;
  But thou art all to me.

Song

Memory, hither come,
  And tune your merry notes;
And, while upon the wind
  Your music floats,
I'll pore upon the stream,
Where sighing lovers dream,
And fish for fancies as they pass
Within the watery glass.

I'll drink of the clear stream,
  And hear the linnet's song;
And there I'll lie and dream
  The day along:
And, when night comes, I'll go
  To places fit for woe,
Walking along the darken'd valley
  With silent Melancholy.

Mad Song

The wild winds weep,
  And the night is a-cold;
Come hither, Sleep,
  And my griefs unfold:
But lo! the morning peeps
  Over the eastern steeps,
And the rustling birds of dawn
The earth do scorn.

Lo! to the vault
  Of paved heaven,

With sorrow fraught
  My notes are driven:
They strike the ear of night,
  Make weep the eyes of day;
They make mad the roaring winds,
  And with tempests play.

Like a fiend in a cloud,
  With howling woe,
After night I do croud,
  And with night will go;
I turn my back to the east,
From whence comforts have increas'd;
For light doth seize my brain
With frantic pain.

Song

Fresh from the dewy hill, the merry year
Smiles on my head, and mounts his flaming car;
Round my young brows the laurel wreathes a shade,
And rising glories beam around my head.

My feet are wing'd, while o'er the dewy lawn
I meet my maiden, risen like the morn:
Oh bless those holy feet, like angels' feet;
Oh bless those limbs, beaming with heav'nly light!

Like as an angel glitt'ring in the sky
In times of innocence and holy joy;
The joyful shepherd stops his grateful song
To hear the music of an angel's tongue.

So when she speaks, the voice of Heaven I hear:
So when we walk, nothing impure comes near;
Each field seems Eden, and each calm retreat;
Each village seems the haunt of holy feet.

But that sweet village, where my black-ey'd maid
Closes her eyes in sleep beneath night's shade,
Whene'er I enter, more than mortal fire
Burns in my soul, and does my song inspire.

Song

When early morn walks forth in sober grey,
Then to my black ey'd maid I haste away;
When evening sits beneath her dusky bow'r,
And gently sighs away the silent hour,
The village bell alarms, away I go,
And the vale darkens at my pensive woe.

To that sweet village, where my black ey'd maid
Doth drop a tear beneath the silent shade,
I turn my eyes; and, pensive as I go,
Curse my black stars, and bless my pleasing woe.

Oft when the summer sleeps among the trees,
Whisp'ring faint murmurs to the scanty breeze,
I walk the village round; if at her side
A youth doth walk in stolen joy and pride,
I curse my stars in bitter grief and woe,
That made my love so high, and me so low.

O should she e'er prove false, his limbs I'd tear,
And throw all pity on the burning air;
I'd curse bright fortune for my mixed lot,
And then I'd die in peace, and be forgot.

To the Muses

Whether on Ida's shady brow,
   Or in the chambers of the East,

[*To the Muses*]

The chambers of the sun, that now
   From antient melody have ceas'd;

Whether in Heav'n ye wander fair,
   Or the green corners of the earth,
Or the blue regions of the air,
   Where the melodious winds have birth;

Whether on chrystal rocks ye rove,
   Beneath the bosom of the sea
Wand'ring in many a coral grove,
   Fair Nine, forsaking Poetry!

How have you left the antient love
   That bards of old enjoy'd in you!
The languid strings do scarcely move!
   The sound is forc'd, the notes are few!

Poems written in a copy of *Poetical Sketches*

SONG 1ST BY A SHEPHERD

Welcome, stranger, to this place,
Where joy doth sit on every bough,
Paleness flies from every face;
We reap not what we do not sow.

Innocence doth like a rose
Bloom on every maiden's cheek;
Honour twines around her brows,
The jewel health adorns her neck.

SONG 2ND BY A YOUNG SHEPHERD

When the trees do laugh with our merry wit,
And the green hill laughs with the noise of it,

When the meadows laugh with lively green
And the grasshopper laughs in the merry scene,

When the greenwood laughs with the voice of joy,
And the dimpling stream runs laughing by,
When Edessa, and Lyca, and Emilie,
With their sweet round mouths sing ha, ha, he,

When the painted Birds laugh in the shade,
Where our table with cherries and nuts is spread;
Come live and be merry and join with me
To sing the sweet chorus of ha, ha, he.

SONG BY AN OLD SHEPHERD

When silver snow decks Sylvio's clothes
And jewel hangs at shepherd's nose,
We can abide life's pelting storm
That makes our limbs quake, if our hearts be warm.

Whilst Virtue is our walking-staff
And Truth a lantern to our path,
We can abide life's pelting storm
That makes our limbs quake, if our hearts be warm.

Blow, boisterous wind, stern winter frown,
Innocence is a winter's gown;
So clad, we'll abide life's pelting storm
That makes our limbs quake, if our hearts be warm.

Songs of Innocence and of Experience

SHEWING THE TWO CONTRARY STATES
OF THE HUMAN SOUL

Songs of Innocence

Introduction

Piping down the valleys wild,
Piping songs of pleasant glee,
On a cloud I saw a child,
And he laughing said to me:

"Pipe a song about a Lamb!"
So I piped with merry chear.
"Piper, pipe that song again;"
So I piped: he wept to hear.

"Drop thy pipe, thy happy pipe;
Sing thy songs of happy chear:"
So I sung the same again,
While he wept with joy to hear.

"Piper, sit thee down and write
In a book, that all may read."
So he vanish'd from my sight,
And I pluck'd a hollow reed,

And I made a rural pen,
And I stain'd the water clear,
And I wrote my happy songs
Every child may joy to hear.

The Shepherd

How sweet is the Shepherd's sweet lot!
From the morn to the evening he strays;
He shall follow his sheep all the day,
And his tongue shall be filled with praise.

For he hears the lamb's innocent call,
And he hears the ewe's tender reply;
He is watchful while they are in peace,
For they know when their Shepherd is nigh.

The Ecchoing Green

The Sun does arise,
And make happy the skies;
The merry bells ring
To welcome the Spring;
The skylark and thrush,
The birds of the bush,
Sing louder around
To the bells' chearful sound,
While our sports shall be seen
On the Ecchoing Green.

Old John, with white hair,
Does laugh away care,
Sitting under the oak,
Among the old folk.
They laugh at our play,
And soon they all say:
"Such, such were the joys
When we all, girls & boys,
In our youth time were seen
On the Ecchoing Green."

Till the little ones, weary,
No more can be merry;
The sun does descend,
And our sports have an end.
Round the laps of their mothers
Many sisters and brothers,
Like birds in their nest,
Are ready for rest,
And sport no more seen
On the darkening Green.

The Lamb

Little Lamb, who made thee?
Dost thou know who made thee?
Gave thee life, & bid thee feed
By the stream & o'er the mead;
Gave thee clothing of delight,
Softest clothing, wooly, bright;
Gave thee such a tender voice,
Making all the vales rejoice?
Little Lamb, who made thee?
Dost thou know who made thee?

Little Lamb, I'll tell thee,
Little Lamb, I'll tell thee:
He is called by thy name,
For he calls himself a Lamb.
He is meek, & he is mild;
He became a little child.
I a child, & thou a lamb,
We are called by his name.
Little Lamb, God bless thee!
Little Lamb, God bless thee!

The Little Black Boy

My mother bore me in the southern wild,
And I am black, but O! my soul is white;
White as an angel is the English child,
But I am black, as if bereav'd of light.

My mother taught me underneath a tree,
And sitting down before the heat of day,
She took me on her lap and kissed me,
And pointing to the east, began to say:

"Look on the rising sun: there God does live,
And gives his light, and gives his heat away;
And flowers and trees and beasts and men receive
Comfort in morning, joy in the noonday.

"And we are put on earth a little space,
That we may learn to bear the beams of love;
And these black bodies and this sunburnt face
Is but a cloud, and like a shady grove.

"For when our souls have learn'd the heat to bear,
The cloud will vanish; we shall hear his voice,
Saying: 'Come out from the grove, my love & care,
And round my golden tent like lambs rejoice.' "

Thus did my mother say, and kissed me;
And thus I say to little English boy:
When I from black and he from white cloud free,
And round the tent of God like lambs we joy,

I'll shade him from the heat, till he can bear
To lean in joy upon our father's knee;
And then I'll stand and stroke his silver hair,
And be like him, and he will then love me.

The Blossom

Merry, Merry Sparrow!
Under leaves so green
A happy Blossom
Sees you swift as arrow
Seek your cradle narrow
Near my Bosom.

Pretty, Pretty Robin!
Under leaves so green
A happy Blossom
Hears you sobbing, sobbing,
Pretty, Pretty Robin,
Near my Bosom.

The Chimney Sweeper

When my mother died I was very young,
And my father sold me while yet my tongue
Could scarcely cry " 'weep! 'weep! 'weep! 'weep!"
So your chimneys I sweep, & in soot I sleep.

There's little Tom Dacre, who cried when his head,
That curl'd like a lamb's back, was shav'd: so I said
"Hush, Tom! never mind it, for when your head's bare
You know that the soot cannot spoil your white hair."

And so he was quiet, & that very night,
As Tom was a-sleeping, he had such a sight!
That thousands of sweepers, Dick, Joe, Ned, & Jack,
Were all of them lock'd up in coffins of black.

And by came an Angel who had a bright key,
And he open'd the coffins & set them all free;
Then down a green plain leaping, laughing, they run,
And wash in a river, and shine in the Sun.

Then naked & white, all their bags left behind,
They rise upon clouds and sport in the wind;
And the Angel told Tom, if he'd be a good boy,
He'd have God for his father, & never want joy.

And so Tom awoke; and we rose in the dark,
And got with our bags & our brushes to work.
Tho' the morning was cold, Tom was happy & warm;
So if all do their duty they need not fear harm.

The Little Boy Lost

"Father! father! where are you going?
O do not walk so fast.
Speak, father, speak to your little boy,
Or else I shall be lost."

The night was dark, no father was there;
The child was wet with dew;
The mire was deep, & the child did weep,
And away the vapour flew.

The Little Boy Found

The little boy lost in the lonely fen,
Led by the wand'ring light,
Began to cry; but God, ever nigh,
Appear'd like his father in white.

He kissed the child & by the hand led
And to his mother brought,
Who in sorrow pale, thro' the lonely dale,
Her little boy weeping sought.

Laughing Song

When the green woods laugh with the voice of joy,
And the dimpling stream runs laughing by;
When the air does laugh with our merry wit,
And the green hill laughs with the noise of it;

When the meadows laugh with lively green,
And the grasshopper laughs in the merry scene,
When Mary and Susan and Emily
With their sweet round mouths sing "Ha, Ha, He!"

When the painted birds laugh in the shade,
Where our table with cherries and nuts is spread,
Come live & be merry, and join with me,
To sing the sweet chorus of "Ha, Ha, He!"

A Cradle Song

Sweet dreams, form a shade
O'er my lovely infant's head;
Sweet dreams of pleasant streams
By happy, silent, moony beams.

Sweet sleep, with soft down
Weave thy brows an infant crown.
Sweet sleep, Angel mild,
Hover o'er my happy child.

Sweet smiles, in the night
Hover over my delight;
Sweet smiles, Mother's smiles,
All the livelong night beguiles.

Sweet moans, dovelike sighs,
Chase not slumber from thy eyes.

Sweet moans, sweeter smiles,
All the dovelike moans beguiles.

Sleep, sleep, happy child,
All creation slept and smil'd;
Sleep, sleep, happy sleep,
While o'er thee thy mother weep.

Sweet babe, in thy face
Holy image I can trace.
Sweet babe, once like thee,
Thy maker lay and wept for me,

Wept for me, for thee, for all,
When he was an infant small.
Thou his image ever see,
Heavenly face that smiles on thee,

Smiles on thee, on me, on all;
Who became an infant small.
Infant smiles are his own smiles;
Heaven & earth to peace beguiles.

The Divine Image

To Mercy, Pity, Peace, and Love
All pray in their distress;
And to these virtues of delight
Return their thankfulness.

For Mercy, Pity, Peace, and Love
Is God, our father dear,
And Mercy, Pity, Peace, and Love
Is Man, his child and care.

For Mercy has a human heart,
Pity a human face,

And Love, the human form divine,
And Peace, the human dress.

Then every man, of every clime,
That prays in his distress,
Prays to the human form divine,
Love, Mercy, Pity, Peace.

And all must love the human form,
In heathen, turk, or jew;
Where Mercy, Love, & Pity dwell
There God is dwelling too.

Holy Thursday

'Twas on a Holy Thursday, their innocent faces clean,
The children walking two & two, in red & blue & green,
Grey-headed beadles walk'd before, with wands as white as snow,
Till into the high dome of Paul's they like Thames' waters flow.

O what a multitude they seem'd, these flowers of London town!
Seated in companies they sit with radiance all their own.
The hum of multitudes was there, but multitudes of lambs,
Thousands of little boys & girls raising their innocent hands.

Now like a mighty wind they raise to heaven the voice of song,
Or like harmonious thunderings the seats of Heaven among.
Beneath them sit the aged men, wise guardians of the poor;
Then cherish pity, lest you drive an angel from your door.

Night

The sun descending in the west,
The evening star does shine;
The birds are silent in their nest,
And I must seek for mine.
The moon like a flower
In heaven's high bower,
With silent delight
Sits and smiles on the night.

Farewell, green fields and happy groves,
Where flocks have took delight.
Where lambs have nibbled, silent moves
The feet of angels bright;
Unseen they pour blessing
And joy without ceasing,
On each bud and blossom,
And each sleeping bosom.

They look in every thoughtless nest,
Where birds are cover'd warm:
They visit caves of every beast,
To keep them all from harm.
If they see any weeping
That should have been sleeping,
They pour sleep on their head,
And sit down by their bed.

When wolves and tygers howl for prey,
They pitying stand and weep;
Seeking to drive their thirst away,
And keep them from the sheep;
But if they rush dreadful,
The angels, most heedful,
Receive each mild spirit,
New worlds to inherit.

And there the lion's ruddy eyes
Shall flow with tears of gold,
And pitying the tender cries,
And walking round the fold,
Saying "Wrath, by his meekness,
And by his health, sickness
Is driven away
From our immortal day.

"And now beside thee, bleating lamb,
I can lie down and sleep;
Or think on him who bore thy name,
Graze after thee and weep.
For, wash'd in life's river,
My bright mane for ever
Shall shine like the gold
As I guard o'er the fold."

Spring

Sound the Flute!
Now it's mute.
Birds delight
Day and Night;
Nightingale
In the dale,
Lark in Sky,
Merrily,
Merrily, Merrily, to welcome in the Year.

Little Boy,
Full of joy;
Little Girl,
Sweet and small;
Cock does crow,
So do you;
Merry voice,

Infant noise,
Merrily, Merrily, to welcome in the Year.

Little Lamb,
Here I am;
Come and lick
My white neck;
Let me pull
Your soft Wool;
Let me kiss
Your soft face:
Merrily, Merrily, we welcome in the Year.

Nurse's Song

When the voices of children are heard on the green
And laughing is heard on the hill,
My heart is at rest within my breast
And everything else is still.

"Then come home, my children, the sun is gone down
And the dews of night arise;
Come, come, leave off play, and let us away
Till the morning appears in the skies."

"No, no, let us play, for it is yet day
And we cannot go to sleep;
Besides, in the sky the little birds fly
And the hills are all cover'd with sheep."

"Well, well, go & play till the light fades away
And then go home to bed."
The little ones leaped & shouted & laugh'd
And all the hills ecchoed.

Infant Joy

"I have no name:
I am but two days old."
What shall I call thee?
"I happy am,
Joy is my name."
Sweet joy befall thee!

Pretty joy!
Sweet joy but two days old,
Sweet joy I call thee:
Thou dost smile,
I sing the while,
Sweet joy befall thee!

A Dream

Once a dream did weave a shade
O'er my Angel-guarded bed,
That an Emmet lost its way
Where on grass methought I lay.

Troubled, 'wilder'd, and forlorn,
Dark, benighted, travel-worn,
Over many a tangled spray,
All heart-broke I heard her say:

"O, my children! do they cry?
Do they hear their father sigh?
Now they look abroad to see:
Now return and weep for me."

Pitying, I drop'd a tear;
But I saw a glow-worm near,
Who replied: "What wailing wight
Calls the watchman of the night?

"I am set to light the ground,
While the beetle goes his round:
Follow now the beetle's hum;
Little wanderer, hie thee home."

On Another's Sorrow

Can I see another's woe,
And not be in sorrow too?
Can I see another's grief,
And not seek for kind relief?

Can I see a falling tear,
And not feel my sorrow's share?
Can a father see his child
Weep, nor be with sorrow fill'd?

Can a mother sit and hear
An infant groan an infant fear?
No, no! never can it be!
Never, never can it be!

And can he who smiles on all
Hear the wren with sorrows small,
Hear the small bird's grief & care,
Hear the woes that infants bear,

And not sit beside the nest,
Pouring pity in their breast;
And not sit the cradle near,
Weeping tear on infant's tear;

And not sit both night & day,
Wiping all our tears away?
O, no! never can it be!
Never, never can it be!

He doth give his joy to all;
He becomes an infant small;
He becomes a man of woe;
He doth feel the sorrow too.

Think not thou canst sigh a sigh
And thy maker is not by;
Think not thou canst weep a tear
And thy maker is not near.

O! he gives to us his joy
That our grief he may destroy;
Till our grief is fled & gone
He doth sit by us and moan.

Songs of Experience

Introduction

Hear the voice of the Bard!
Who Present, Past, & Future, sees;
Whose ears have heard
The Holy Word
That walk'd among the ancient trees,

Calling the lapsed Soul,
And weeping in the evening dew;
That might controll
The starry pole,
And fallen, fallen light renew!

"O Earth, O Earth, return!
Arise from out the dewy grass;
Night is worn,
And the morn
Rises from the slumberous mass.

"Turn away no more;
Why wilt thou turn away?
The starry floor,
The wat'ry shore,
Is giv'n thee till the break of day."

Earth's Answer

Earth rais'd up her head
From the darkness dread & drear.
Her light fled,
Stony dread!
And her locks cover'd with grey despair.

"Prison'd on wat'ry shore,
Starry Jealousy does keep my den:
Cold and hoar,
Weeping o'er,
I hear the father of the ancient men.

"Selfish father of men!
Cruel, jealous, selfish fear!
Can delight,
Chain'd in night,
The virgins of youth and morning bear?

"Does spring hide its joy
When buds and blossoms grow?
Does the sower
Sow by night,
Or the plowman in darkness plow?

"Break this heavy chain
That does freeze my bones around.
Selfish! vain!
Eternal bane!
That free Love with bondage bound."

The Clod and the Pebble

"Love seeketh not Itself to please,
Nor for itself hath any care,
But for another gives its ease,
And builds a Heaven in Hell's despair."

So sung a little Clod of Clay
Trodden with the cattle's feet,
But a Pebble of the brook
Warbled out these metres meet:

"Love seeketh only Self to please,
To bind another to Its delight,
Joys in another's loss of ease,
And builds a Hell in Heaven's despite."

Holy Thursday

Is this a holy thing to see
In a rich and fruitful land,
Babes reduc'd to misery,
Fed with cold and usurous hand?

Is that trembling cry a song?
Can it be a song of joy?
And so many children poor?
It is a land of poverty!

And their sun does never shine,
And their fields are bleak & bare,
And their ways are fill'd with thorns:
It is eternal winter there.

For where-e'er the sun does shine,
And where-e'er the rain does fall,

Babe can never hunger there,
Nor poverty the mind appall.

The Little Girl Lost

In futurity
I prophetic see
That the earth from sleep
(Grave the sentence deep)

Shall arise and seek
For her maker meek;
And the desart wild
Become a garden mild.

*   *   *   *

In the southern clime,
Where the summer's prime
Never fades away,
Lovely Lyca lay.

Seven summers old
Lovely Lyca told;
She had wander'd long
Hearing wild birds' song.

"Sweet sleep, come to me
Underneath this tree.
Do father, mother weep,
Where can Lyca sleep?

"Lost in desart wild
Is your little child.
How can Lyca sleep
If her mother weep?

[*The Little Girl Lost*]

"If her heart does ake
Then let Lyca wake;
If my mother sleep,
Lyca shall not weep.

"Frowning, frowning night,
O'er this desart bright
Let thy moon arise
While I close my eyes."

Sleeping Lyca lay
While the beasts of prey,
Come from caverns deep,
View'd the maid asleep.

The kingly lion stood
And the virgin view'd,
Then he gamboll'd round
O'er the hallow'd ground.

Leopards, tygers, play
Round her as she lay,
While the lion old
Bow'd his mane of gold

And her bosom lick,
And upon her neck
From his eyes of flame
Ruby tears there came;

While the lioness
Loos'd her slender dress,
And naked they convey'd
To caves the sleeping maid.

The Little Girl Found

All the night in woe
Lyca's parents go
Over vallies deep,
While the desarts weep.

Tired and woe-begone,
Hoarse with making moan,
Arm in arm seven days
They trac'd the desart ways.

Seven nights they sleep
Among shadows deep,
And dream they see their child
Starv'd in desart wild.

Pale, thro' pathless ways
The fancied image strays
Famish'd, weeping, weak,
With hollow piteous shriek.

Rising from unrest,
The trembling woman prest
With feet of weary woe:
She could no further go.

In his arms he bore
Her, arm'd with sorrow sore;
Till before their way
A couching lion lay.

Turning back was vain:
Soon his heavy mane
Bore them to the ground.
Then he stalk'd around,

Smelling to his prey;
But their fears allay
When he licks their hands,
And silent by them stands.

They look upon his eyes
Fill'd with deep surprise,
And wondering behold
A spirit arm'd in gold.

On his head a crown,
On his shoulders down
Flow'd his golden hair.
Gone was all their care.

"Follow me," he said;
"Weep not for the maid;
In my palace deep
Lyca lies asleep."

Then they followed
Where the vision led,
And saw their sleeping child
Among tygers wild.

To this day they dwell
In a lonely dell;
Nor fear the wolvish howl
Nor the lions' growl.

The Chimney Sweeper

A little black thing among the snow,
Crying ' 'weep! 'weep!' in notes of woe!
"Where are thy father & mother? say?"
"They are both gone up to the church to pray.

"Because I was happy upon the heath,
And smil'd among the winter's snow,
They clothed me in the clothes of death,
And taught me to sing the notes of woe.

"And because I am happy & dance & sing,
They think they have done me no injury,
And are gone to praise God & his Priest & King,
Who make up a heaven of our misery."

Nurse's Song

When the voices of children are heard on the green
And whisp'rings are in the dale,
The days of my youth rise fresh in my mind,
My face turns green and pale.

Then come home, my children, the sun is gone down,
And the dews of night arise;
Your spring & your day are wasted in play,
And your winter and night in disguise.

The Sick Rose

O Rose, thou art sick!
The invisible worm
That flies in the night,
In the howling storm,

Has found out thy bed
Of crimson joy,
And his dark secret love
Does thy life destroy.

The Fly

Little Fly,
Thy summer's play
My thoughtless hand
Has brush'd away.

Am not I
A fly like thee?
Or art not thou
A man like me?

For I dance,
And drink, & sing,
Till some blind hand
Shall brush my wing.

If thought is life
And strength & breath,
And the want
Of thought is death;

Then am I
A happy fly,
If I live
Or if I die.

The Angel

I dreamt a Dream! what can it mean?
And that I was a maiden Queen,
Guarded by an Angel mild:
Witless woe was ne'er beguil'd!

And I wept both night and day,
And he wip'd my tears away,

And I wept both day and night,
And hid from him my heart's delight.

So he took his wings and fled;
Then the morn blush'd rosy red;
I dried my tears, & arm'd my fears
With ten thousand shields and spears.

Soon my Angel came again:
I was arm'd, he came in vain;
For the time of youth was fled,
And grey hairs were on my head.

The Tyger

Tyger! Tyger! burning bright
In the forests of the night,
What immortal hand or eye
Could frame thy fearful symmetry?

In what distant deeps or skies
Burnt the fire of thine eyes?
On what wings dare he aspire?
What the hand dare sieze the fire?

And what shoulder, & what art,
Could twist the sinews of thy heart?
And when thy heart began to beat,
What dread hand? & what dread feet?

What the hammer? what the chain?
In what furnace was thy brain?
What the anvil? what dread grasp
Dare its deadly terrors clasp?

When the stars threw down their spears,
And water'd heaven with their tears,

Did he smile his work to see?
Did he who made the Lamb make thee?

Tyger! Tyger! burning bright
In the forests of the night,
What immortal hand or eye,
Dare frame thy fearful symmetry?

My Pretty Rose-tree

A flower was offer'd to me,
Such a flower as May never bore;
But I said "I've a Pretty Rose-tree,"
And I passed the sweet flower o'er.

Then I went to my Pretty Rose-tree,
To tend her by day and by night;
But my Rose turn'd away with jealousy,
And her thorns were my only delight.

Ah! Sun-flower

Ah, Sun-flower! weary of time,
Who countest the steps of the Sun,
Seeking after that sweet golden clime
Where the traveller's journey is done:

Where the Youth pined away with desire,
And the pale Virgin shrouded in snow
Arise from their graves, and aspire
Where my Sun-flower wishes to go.

The Lilly

The modest Rose puts forth a thorn,

The humble Sheep a threat'ning horn;
While the Lilly white shall in Love delight,
Nor a thorn, nor a threat, stain her beauty bright.

The Garden of Love

I went to the Garden of Love,
And saw what I never had seen:
A Chapel was built in the midst,
Where I used to play on the green.

And the gates of this Chapel were shut,
And "Thou shalt not" writ over the door;
So I turn'd to the Garden of Love
That so many sweet flowers bore;

And I saw it was filled with graves,
And tomb-stones where flowers should be;
And Priests in black gowns were walking their rounds,
And binding with briars my joys & desires.

The Little Vagabond

Dear Mother, dear Mother, the Church is cold,
But the Ale-house is healthy & pleasant & warm;
Besides I can tell where I am used well,
Such usage in Heaven will never do well.
But if at the Church they would give us some Ale,
And a pleasant fire our souls to regale,
We'd sing and we'd pray all the live-long day,
Nor ever once wish from the Church to stray.

Then the Parson might preach, & drink, & sing,
And we'd be as happy as birds in the spring;
And modest Dame Lurch, who is always at Church,
Would not have bandy children, nor fasting, nor birch.

And God, like a father rejoicing to see
His children as pleasant and happy as he,
Would have no more quarrel with the Devil or the Barrel,
But kiss him, & give him both drink and apparel.

London

I wander thro' each charter'd street,
Near where the charter'd Thames does flow,
And mark in every face I meet
Marks of weakness, marks of woe.

In every cry of every Man,
In every Infant's cry of fear,
In every voice, in every ban,
The mind-forg'd manacles I hear.

How the Chimney-sweeper's cry
Every black'ning Church appalls;
And the hapless Soldier's sigh
Runs in blood down Palace walls.

But most thro' midnight streets I hear
How the youthful Harlot's curse
Blasts the new born Infant's tear,
And blights with plagues the Marriage hearse.

The Human Abstract

Pity would be no more
If we did not make somebody Poor;
And Mercy no more could be
If all were as happy as we.

And mutual fear brings peace,
Till the selfish loves increase:

Then Cruelty knits a snare,
And spreads his baits with care.

He sits down with holy fears,
And waters the ground with tears;
Then Humility takes its root
Underneath his foot.

Soon spreads the dismal shade
Of Mystery over his head;
And the Catterpiller and Fly
Feed on the Mystery.

And it bears the fruit of Deceit,
Ruddy and sweet to eat;
And the Raven his nest has made
In its thickest shade.

The Gods of the earth and sea
Sought thro' Nature to find this Tree;
But their search was all in vain:
There grows one in the Human Brain.

A Poison Tree

I was angry with my friend:
I told my wrath, my wrath did end.
I was angry with my foe:
I told it not, my wrath did grow.

And I water'd it in fears,
Night & morning with my tears;
And I sunned it with smiles,
And with soft deceitful wiles.

And it grew both day and night,
Till it bore an apple bright;

And my foe beheld it shine,
And he knew that it was mine,

And into my garden stole
When the night had veil'd the pole:
In the morning glad I see
My foe outstretch'd beneath the tree.

A Little Boy Lost

"Nought loves another as itself,
Nor venerates another so,
Nor is it possible to Thought
A greater than itself to know:

"And Father, how can I love you
Or any of my brothers more?
I love you like the little bird
That picks up crumbs around the door."

The Priest sat by and heard the child,
In trembling zeal he siez'd his hair:
He led him by his little coat,
And all admir'd the Priestly care.

And standing on the altar high,
"Lo! what a fiend is here!" said he,
"One who sets reason up for judge
Of our most holy Mystery."

The weeping child could not be heard,
The weeping parents wept in vain;
They strip'd him to his little shirt,
And bound him in an iron chain;

And burn'd him in a holy place,
Where many had been burn'd before:

The weeping parents wept in vain.
Are such things done on Albion's shore?

A Little Girl Lost

Children of the future Age
Reading this indignant page,
Know that in a former time
Love! sweet Love! was thought a crime.

In the Age of Gold,
Free from winter's cold,
Youth and maiden bright
To the holy light,
Naked in the sunny beams delight.

Once a youthful pair,
Fill'd with softest care,
Met in garden bright
Where the holy light
Had just remov'd the curtains of the night.

There, in rising day,
On the grass they play;
Parents were afar,
Strangers came not near,
And the maiden soon forgot her fear.

Tired with kisses sweet,
They agree to meet
When the silent sleep
Waves o'er heaven's deep,
And the weary tired wanderers weep.

To her father white
Came the maiden bright;
But his loving look,

Like the holy book,
All her tender limbs with terror shook.

"Ona! pale and weak!
To thy father speak:
O, the trembling fear!
O, the dismal care!
That shakes the blossoms of my hoary hair."

To Tirzah

Whate'er is Born of Mortal Birth
Must be consumed with the Earth
To rise from Generation free:
Then what have I to do with thee?

The Sexes sprung from Shame & Pride,
Blow'd in the morn; in evening died;
But Mercy chang'd Death into Sleep;
The Sexes rose to work & weep.

Thou, Mother of my Mortal part,
With cruelty didst mould my Heart,
And with false self-decieving tears
Didst bind my Nostrils, Eyes, & Ears:

Didst close my Tongue in senseless clay,
And me to Mortal Life betray.
The Death of Jesus set me free:
Then what have I to do with thee?

The Schoolboy

I love to rise in a summer morn
When the birds sing on every tree;
The distant huntsman winds his horn,

And the sky-lark sings with me.
O! what sweet company.

But to go to school in a summer morn,
O! it drives all joy away;
Under a cruel eye outworn,
The little ones spend the day
In sighing and dismay.

Ah! then at times I drooping sit,
And spend many an anxious hour,
Nor in my book can I take delight,
Nor sit in learning's bower,
Worn thro' with the dreary shower.

How can the bird that is born for joy
Sit in a cage and sing?
How can a child, when fears annoy,
But droop his tender wing,
And forget his youthful spring?

O! father & mother, if buds are nip'd
And blossoms blown away,
And if the tender plants are strip'd
Of their joy in the springing day,
By sorrow and care's dismay,

How shall the summer arise in joy,
Or the summer fruits appear?
Or how shall we gather what griefs destroy,
Or bless the mellowing year,
When the blasts of winter appear?

The Voice of the Ancient Bard

Youth of delight, come hither,
And see the opening morn,

Image of truth new born.
Doubt is fled, & clouds of reason,
Dark disputes & artful teazing.
Folly is an endless maze,
Tangled roots perplex her ways.
How many have fallen there!
They stumble all night over bones of the dead,
And feel they know not what but care,
And wish to lead others, when they should be led.

A Divine Image

Cruelty has a Human Heart,
And Jealousy a Human Face;
Terror the Human Form Divine,
And Secrecy the Human Dress.

The Human Dress is forged Iron,
The Human Form a fiery Forge,
The Human Face a Furnace seal'd,
The Human Heart its hungry Gorge.

Poems from the Rossetti MS

◆

Never seek to tell thy love
Love that never told can be;
For the gentle wind does move
Silently, invisibly.

I told my love, I told my love,
I told her all my heart,
Trembling, cold, in ghastly fears—
Ah, she doth depart.

Soon as she was gone from me
A traveller came by
Silently, invisibly—
O, was no deny.

◆

I asked a thief to steal me a peach:
He turned up his eyes.
I ask'd a lithe lady to lie her down:
Holy & meek she cries—

As soon as I went
An angel came.
He wink'd at the thief
And smil'd at the dame.

And without one word said
Had a peach from the tree
And still as a maid
Enjoy'd the lady.

A Cradle Song

Sleep, Sleep, beauty bright
Dreaming o'er the joys of night.
Sleep, Sleep: in thy sleep
Little sorrows sit & weep.

Sweet Babe, in thy face
Soft desires I can trace
Secret joys & secret smiles
Little pretty infant wiles.

As thy softest limbs I feel
Smiles as of the morning steal

Infant Sorrow

My mother groan'd, my father wept;
Into the dangerous world I leapt,
Helpless, naked, piping loud,
Like a fiend hid in a cloud.

Struggling in my father's hands
Striving against my swaddling bands,
Bound & weary, I thought best
To sulk upon my mother's breast.
When I saw that rage was vain,
And to sulk would nothing gain,
O'er thy cheek & o'er thy breast
Where thy little heart does rest.

O, the cunning wiles that creep
In thy little heart asleep.
When thy little heart does wake,
Then the dreadful lightnings break.

From thy cheek & from thy eye
O'er the youthful harvests nigh
Infant wiles & infant smiles
Heaven & Earth of peace beguiles.

◆

Turning many a trick & wile,
I began to soothe & smile.

And I sooth'd day after day
Till upon the ground I stray;
And I smil'd night after night,
Seeking only for delight.

And I saw before me shine
Clusters of the wand'ring vine,

And many a lovely flower & tree
Stretch'd their blossoms out to me.

My father then with holy look,
In his hands a holy book,
Pronounc'd curses on my head
And bound me in a mirtle shade.

In a Mirtle Shade

Why should I be bound to thee,
O my lovely mirtle tree?
Love, free love, cannot be bound
To any tree that grows on ground.

O, how sick & weary I
Underneath my mirtle lie,
Like to dung upon the ground
Underneath my mirtle bound.

Oft my mirtle sigh'd in vain
To behold my heavy chain;
Oft my father saw us sigh,
And laugh'd at our simplicity.

So I smote him & his gore
Stain'd the roots my mirtle bore.
But the time of youth is fled,
And grey hairs are on my head.

◆

O lapwing, thou fliest around the heath,
Nor seest the net that is spread beneath.
Why dost thou not fly among the corn fields?
They cannot spread nets where a harvest yields.

◆

Thou hast a lap full of seed,
And this is a fine country.
Why dost thou not cast thy seed
And live in it merrily?

Shall I cast it on the sand
And turn it into fruitful land?
For on no other ground
Can I sow my seed
Without tearing up
Some stinking weed.

To Nobodaddy

Why art thou silent & invisible,
Father of Jealousy?
Why dost thou hide thy self in clouds
From every searching Eye?

Why darkness & obscurity
In all thy words & laws,
That none dare eat the fruit but from
The wily serpent's jaws?
Or is it because Secresy gains females' loud applause?

◆

Are not the joys of morning sweeter
Than the joys of night?
And are the vig'rous joys of youth
Ashamed of the light?

Let age & sickness silent rob
The vineyards in the night;

But those who burn with vig'rous youth
Pluck fruits before the light.

◆

Love to faults is always blind,
Always is to joy inclin'd,
Lawless, wing'd, & unconfin'd,
And breaks all chains from every mind.

Deceit to secresy confin'd,
Lawful, cautious, & refin'd;
To every thing but interest blind,
And forges fetters for the mind.

The Wild Flower's Song

As I wander'd the forest,
The green leaves among,
I heard a wild flower
Singing a song:

"I slept in the dark
In the silent night,
I murmur'd my fears
And I felt delight.

"In the morning I went
As rosy as morn
To seek for new Joy,
But I met with scorn."

Soft Snow

I walked abroad in a snowy day:
I ask'd the soft snow with me to play:

She play'd & she melted in all her prime,
And the winter call'd it a dreadful crime.

An Ancient Proverb

Remove away that black'ning church:
Remove away that marriage hearse:
Remove away that place of blood:
You'll quite remove the ancient curse.

To My Mirtle

To a lovely mirtle bound,
Blossoms show'ring all around,
Oh, how sick & weary I
Underneath my mirtle lie.
Why should I be bound to thee,
O, my lovely mirtle tree?

Merlin's Prophecy

The harvest shall flourish in wintry weather
When two virginities meet together:

The King & the Priest must be tied in a tether
Before two virgins can meet together.

◆

The sword sung on the barren heath,
The sickle in the fruitful field:
The sword he sung a song of death,
But could not make the sickle yield.

◆

Abstinence sows sand all over
The ruddy limbs & flaming hair,
But Desire Gratified
Plants fruits of life & beauty there.

◆

In a wife I would desire
What in whores is always found—
The lineaments of Gratified desire.

Eternity

He who binds to himself a joy
Does the winged life destroy;
But he who kisses the joy as it flies
Lives in eternity's sun rise.

The Question Answer'd

What is it men in women do require?
The lineaments of Gratified Desire.
What is it women do in men require?
The lineaments of Gratified Desire.

Motto to the Songs of Innocence & of Experience

The Good are attracted by Men's perceptions,
And think not for themselves;
Till Experience teaches them to catch
And to cage the Fairies & Elves.

And then the Knave begins to snarl
And the Hypocrite to howl;
And all his good Friends shew their private ends,
And the Eagle is known from the Owl.

◆

"Let the Brothels of Paris be opened
With many an alluring dance
To awake the Pestilence thro' the city,"
Said the beautiful Queen of France.

The King awoke on his couch of gold,
As soon as he heard these tidings told:
"Arise & come, both fife & drum,
And the Famine shall eat both crust & crumb."

Then he swore a great & solemn Oath:
"To kill the people I am loth,
But If they rebel, they must go to hell:
They shall have a Priest & a passing bell."

Then old Nobodaddy aloft
Farted & belch'd & cough'd,
And said, "I love hanging & drawing & quartering
Every bit as well as war & slaughtering.
Damn praying & singing,
Unless they will bring in
The blood of ten thousand by fighting or swinging."

The Queen of France just touched this Globe,
And the Pestilence darted from her robe;
But our good Queen quite grows to the ground,
And a great many suckers grow all around.

Fayette beside King Lewis stood;
He saw him sign his hand;

And soon he saw the famine rage
About the fruitful land.

Fayette beheld the Queen to smile
And wink her lovely eye;
And soon he saw the pestilence
From street to street to fly.

Fayette beheld the King & Queen
In tears & iron bound;
But mute Fayette wept tear for tear,
And guarded them around.

Fayette, Fayette, thou'rt bought & sold,
And sold is thy happy morrow;
Thou gavest the tears of Pity away
In exchange for the tears of sorrow.

Who will exchange his own fire side
For the steps of another's door?
Who will exchange his wheaten loaf
For the links of a dungeon floor?

O, who would smile on the wintry seas,
& Pity the stormy roar?
Or who will exchange his new born child
For the dog at the wintry door?

◆

When Klopstock England defied,
Uprose William Blake in his pride;
For old Nobodaddy aloft
Farted & Belch'd & cough'd;
Then swore a great oath that made heaven quake,
And call'd aloud to English Blake.
Blake was giving his body ease

At Lambeth beneath the poplar trees.
From his seat then started he,
And turned him round three times three.
The Moon at that sight blush'd scarlet red,
The stars threw down their cups & fled,
And all the devils that were in hell
Answered with a ninefold yell.
Klopstock felt the intripled turn,
And all his bowels began to churn,
And his bowels turned round three times three,
And lock'd in his soul with a ninefold key,
That from his body it ne'er could be parted
Till to the last trumpet it was farted.
Then again old Nobodaddy swore
He ne'er had seen such a thing before,
Since Noah was shut in the ark,
Since Eve first chose her hellfire spark,
Since 'twas the fashion to go naked,
Since the old anything was created,
And so feeling, he beg'd me to turn again
And ease poor Klopstock's ninefold pain.
If Blake could do this when he rose up from a shite,
What might he not do if he sat down to write?

◆

A fairy leapt upon my knee
Singing & dancing merrily;
I said, "Thou thing of patches, rings,
Pins, Necklaces, & such like things,
Disguiser of the Female Form,
Thou paltry, gilded, poisonous worm!"
Weeping, he fell upon my thigh,
And thus in tears did soft reply:
"Knowest thou not, O Fairies' Lord!
How much by us Contemn'd, Abhorr'd,
Whatever hides the Female form

That cannot bear the Mental storm?
Therefore in Pity still we give
Our lives to make the Female live;
And what would turn into disease
We turn to what will joy & please."

◆

When a Man has Married a Wife, he finds out whether
Her knees & elbows are only glewed together.

◆

Mock on, Mock on Voltaire, Rousseau:
Mock on, Mock on: 'tis all in vain!
You throw the sand against the wind,
And the wind blows it back again.

And every sand becomes a Gem
Reflected in the beams divine;
Blown back they blind the mocking Eye,
But still in Israel's paths they shine.

The Atoms of Democritus
And Newton's Particles of light
Are sands upon the Red sea shore,
Where Israel's tents do shine so bright.

Morning

To find the Western path
Right thro' the Gates of Wrath
I urge my way;
Sweet Mercy leads me on:

With soft repentant moan
I see the break of day.

The war of swords & spears
Melted by dewy tears
Exhales on high;
The Sun is freed from fears
And with soft grateful tears
Ascends the sky.

◆

Each Man is in his Spectre's power
Untill the arrival of that hour,
When his Humanity awake
And cast his own Spectre into the Lake.

To the Queen

The Door of Death is made of Gold,
That Mortal Eyes cannot behold;
But, when the Mortal Eyes are clos'd,
And cold and pale the Limbs repos'd,
The Soul awakes; and, wond'ring, sees
In her mild Hand the golden Keys:
The Grave is Heaven's Golden Gate,
And rich and poor around it wait;
O Shepherdess of England's Fold,
Behold this Gate of Pearl and Gold!
To dedicate to England's Queen
The Visions that my Soul has seen,
And, by Her kind permission, bring
What I have borne on solemn Wing
From the vast regions of the Grave,
Before Her Throne my Wings I wave;
Bowing before my Sov'reign's Feet,

"The Grave produc'd these Blossoms sweet
In mild repose from Earthly strife;
The Blossoms of Eternal Life!"

◆

The Angel that presided o'er my birth
Said, "Little creature, form'd of Joy & Mirth,
Go love without the help of any Thing on Earth."

◆

Grown old in Love from Seven till Seven times Seven,
I oft have wish'd for Hell for Ease from Heaven.

◆

Why was Cupid a Boy
And why a boy was he?
He should have been a Girl
For ought that I can see.

For he shoots with his bow,
And the Girl shoots with her Eye,
And they both are merry & glad
And laugh when we do cry.

And to make Cupid a Boy
Was the Cupid Girl's mocking plan;
For a boy can't interpret the thing
Till he is become a man.

And then he's so pierc'd with cares
And wounded with arrowy smarts,

That the whole business of his life
Is to pick out the heads of the darts.

'Twas the Greeks' love of war
Turn'd Love into a Boy,
And Woman into a Statue of Stone—
And away flew every Joy.

◆

Since all the Riches of this World
May be gifts from the Devil & Earthly Kings,
I should suspect that I worship'd the Devil
If I thank'd my God for Worldly things.

◆

Nail his neck to the Cross: nail it with a nail.
Nail his neck to the Cross: ye all have power over his tail.

◆

The Caverns of the Grave I've seen,
And these I shew'd to England's Queen.
But now the Caves of Hell I view:
Who shall I dare to shew them to?
What mighty Soul in Beauty's form
Shall dauntless View the Infernal Storm?
Egremont's Countess can controll
The flames of Hell that round me roll.
If she refuse, I still go on
Till the Heavens & Earth are gone,
Still admir'd by Noble minds,
Follow'd by Envy on the winds,
Re-engrav'd Time after Time,

—

Ever in their youthful prime,
My designs unchang'd remain.
Time may rage but rage in vain.
Far above Time's troubled Fountains
On the Great Atlantic Mountains,
In my Golden House on high,
There they Shine Eternally.

◆

I rose up at the dawn of day—
Get thee away! get thee away!
Pray'st thou for Riches? away! away!
This is the Throne of Mammon grey.

Said I, "this sure is very odd.
I took it to be the Throne of God.
For every Thing besides I have:
It is only for Riches that I can crave.

"I have Mental Joy & Mental Health
And Mental Friends & Mental wealth;
I've a Wife I love & that loves me;
I've all but Riches Bodily.

"I am in God's presence night & day,
And he never turns his face away.
The accuser of sins by my side does stand
And he holds my money bag in his hand.

"For my worldly things God makes him pay,
And he'd pay more if to him I would pray;
And so you may do the worst you can do:
Be assur'd Mr. devil I won't pray to you.

"Then If for Riches I must not Pray,
God knows I little of Prayers need say.

So as a Church is known by its Steeple,
If I pray it must be for other People.

"He says, if I do not worship him for a God,
I shall eat coarser food & go worse shod;
So as I don't value such things as these,
You must do, Mr. devil, just as God please."

Miscellaneous Epigrams and Fragments

◆

You don't believe—I won't attempt to make ye:
You are asleep—I won't attempt to wake ye.
Sleep on, Sleep on! while in your pleasant dreams
Of Reason you may drink of Life's clear streams.
Reason and Newton, they are quite two things;
For so the Swallow & the Sparrow sings.
Reason says "Miracle": Newton says "Doubt".
Aye! that's the way to make all Nature out.
"Doubt, Doubt, & don't believe without experiment":
That is the very thing that Jesus meant,
When he said, "Only Believe! Believe & try!
Try, Try, and never mind the Reason why."

◆

Anger & Wrath my bosom rends:
I thought them the Errors of friends.
But all my limbs with warmth glow:
I find them the Errors of the foe.

◆

"Madman" I have been call'd: "Fool" they call thee:
I wonder which they Envy, Thee or Me?

To F[laxman]

I mock thee not, tho' I by thee am Mocked.
Thou call'st me Madman, but I call thee Blockhead.

◆

S[tothard] in Childhood on the Nursery floor
Was extreme Old & most extremely poor.
He is grown old & rich & what he will:
He is extreme old & extreme poor still.

To Nancy F[laxman]

How can I help thy Husband's copying Me?
Should that make difference 'twixt me & Thee?

◆

Of H[ayley]'s birth this was the happy lot,
His Mother on his Father him begot.

◆

He's a Blockhead who wants a proof of what he can't Percieve,
And he's a Fool who tries to make such a Blockhead believe.

◆

Cr[omek] loves artists as he loves his Meat.
He loves the Art, but 'tis the Art to Cheat.

◆

A Petty Sneaking Knave I knew—
O Mr. Cr[omek], how do ye do?

To S[tothar]D

You all your Youth observ'd the Golden Rule
Till you're at last become the golden fool.
I sport with Fortune, Merry, Blithe & Gay,
Like to the Lion Sporting with his Prey.
Take you the hide & horns which you may wear:
Mine is the flesh—the bones may be your Share.

◆

To forgive Enemies H[ayley] does pretend,
Who never in his Life forgave a friend.

On H[ayley]'s Friendship

When H[ayley] finds out what you cannot do,
That is the very thing he'll set you to.
If you break not your Neck, 'tis not his fault,
But pecks of poison arc not pecks of salt.
And when he could not act upon my wife
Hired a Villain to bereave my Life.

Imitation of Pope: a Compliment to the Ladies

Wondrous the Gods, more wondrous are the Men,
More Wondrous Wondrous still the Cock & Hen,
More Wondrous still the Table, Stool & Chair;
But Ah! More wondrous still the Charming Fair.

To H[ayley]

Thy Friendship oft has made my heart to ake:
Do be my Enemy for Friendship's sake.

◆

Here lies John Trot, the Friend of all mankind:
He has not left one Enemy behind.
Friends were quite hard to find, old authors say;
But now they stand in every bodies way.

◆

My title as a Genius thus is prov'd:
Not Prais'd by Hayley nor by Flaxman lov'd.

◆

I, Rubens, am a Statesman & a Saint.
Deceptions? And so I'll learn to Paint.

On H[ayley] the Pick Thank

I write the Rascal Thanks till he & I
With Thanks & Compliments are quite drawn dry.

Cromek Speaks

I always take my judgment from a Fool
Because his judgment is so very Cool,
Not prejudic'd by feelings great or small.
Amiable state! he cannot feel at all.

◆

You say their Pictures well Painted be,
And yet they are Blockheads you all agree.
Thank God, I never was sent to school
To be Flog'd into following the Style of a Fool.

The Errors of a Wise Man make your Rule
Rather than the Perfections of a Fool.

◆

Great things are done when Men & Mountains meet;
This is not done by Jostling in the Street.

◆

If you play a Game of Chance, know, before you begin;
If you are benevolent you will never win.

◆

The only Man that e'er I knew
Who did not make me almost spew
Was Fuseli: he was both Turk & Jew—
And so, dear Christian Friends, how do you do?

To God

If you have form'd a Circle to go into,
Go into it yourself & see how you would do.

Poems from the *Pickering MS*

The Golden Net

Three Virgins at the break of day:
"Whither, young Man, whither away?
Alas for woe! alas for woe!"
They cry, & tears for ever flow.
The one was Cloth'd in flames of fire,
The other Cloth'd in iron wire,
The other Cloth'd in tears & sighs
Dazling bright before my Eyes.
They bore a Net of golden twine
To hang upon the branches fine.
Pitying I wept to see the woe
That Love & Beauty undergo,
To be consum'd in burning Fires
And in ungratified desires,
And in tears cloth'd Night & day
Melted all my Soul away.
When they saw my Tears, a Smile
That did Heaven itself beguile,
Bore the Golden Net aloft
As on downy Pinions soft
Over the Morning of my day.
Underneath the Net I stray,
Now intreating Burning Fire,
Now intreating Iron Wire,
Now intreating Tears & Sighs.
O when will the morning rise?

The Mental Traveller

I travel'd thro' a Land of Men,
A Land of Men & Women too,

And heard & saw such dreadful things
As cold Earth wanderers never knew.

For there the Babe is born in joy
That was begotten in dire woe;
Just as we Reap in joy the fruit
Which we in bitter tears did sow.

And if the Babe is born a Boy
He's given to a Woman Old,
Who nails him down upon a rock,
Catches his shrieks in cups of gold.

She binds iron thorns around his head,
She pierces both his hands & feet,
She cuts his heart out at his side
To make it feel both cold & heat.

Her fingers number every Nerve,
Just as a Miser counts his gold;
She lives upon his shrieks & cries,
And she grows young as he grows old.

Till he becomes a bleeding youth,
And she becomes a Virgin bright;
Then he rends up his Manacles
And binds her down for his delight.

He plants himself in all her Nerves,
Just as a Husbandman his mould;
And she becomes his dwelling place
And Garden fruitful seventy fold.

An aged Shadow, soon he fades,
Wand'ring round an Earthly Cot,
Full filled all with gems & gold
Which he by industry had got.

[*The Mental Traveller*]

And these are the gems of the Human Soul,
The rubies & pearls of a lovesick eye,
The countless gold of the akeing heart,
The martyr's groan & the lover's sigh.

They are his meat, they are his drink;
He feeds the Beggar & the Poor
And the wayfaring Traveller:
For ever open is his door.

His grief is their eternal joy;
They make the roofs & walls to ring;
Till from the fire on the hearth
A little Female Babe does spring.

And she is all of solid fire
And gems & gold, that none his hand
Dares stretch to touch her Baby form,
Or wrap her in his swaddling-band.

But She comes to the Man she loves,
If young or old, or rich or poor;
They soon drive out the aged Host,
A Beggar at another's door.

He wanders weeping far away,
Untill some other take him in;
Oft blind & age-bent, sore distrest,
Untill he can a Maiden win.

And to allay his freezing Age
The Poor Man takes her in his arms;
The Cottage fades before his sight,
The Garden & its lovely Charms.

The Guests are scatter'd thro' the land,
For the Eye altering alters all;

The Senses roll themselves in fear,
And the flat Earth becomes a Ball;

The stars, sun, Moon, all shrink away,
A desart vast without a bound,
And nothing left to eat or drink,
And a dark desart all around.

The honey of her Infant lips,
The bread & wine of her sweet smile,
The wild game of her roving Eye,
Does him to Infancy beguile;

For as he eats & drinks he grows
Younger & younger every day;
And on the desart wild they both
Wander in terror & dismay.

Like the wild Stag she flees away,
Her fear plants many a thicket wild;
While he pursues her night & day,
By various arts of Love beguil'd,

By various arts of Love & Hate,
Till the wide desart planted o'er
With Labyrinths of wayward Love,
Where roam the Lion, Wolf & Boar,

Till he becomes a wayward Babe,
And she a weeping Woman Old.
Then many a Lover wanders here;
The Sun & Stars are nearer roll'd.

The trees bring forth sweet Extacy
To all who in the desart roam;
Till many a City there is Built,
And many a pleasant Shepherd's home.

But when they find the frowning Babe,
Terror strikes thro' the region wide:
They cry "The Babe! the Babe is Born!"
And flee away on Every side.

For who dare touch the frowning form,
His arm is wither'd to its root;
Lions, Boars, Wolves, all howling flee,
And every Tree does shed its fruit.

And none can touch that frowning form,
Except it be a Woman Old;
She nails him down upon the Rock,
And all is done as I have told.

Mary

Sweet Mary, the first time she ever was there,
Came into the Ball room among the Fair;
The young Men & Maidens around her throng,
And these are the words upon every tongue:

"An Angel is here from the heavenly climes,
Or again does return the golden times;
Her eyes outshine every brilliant ray,
She opens her lips—'tis the Month of May."

Mary moves in soft beauty & conscious delight
To augment with sweet smiles all the joys of the Night,
Nor once blushes to own to the rest of the Fair
That sweet Love & Beauty are worthy our care.

In the Morning the Villagers rose with delight
And repeated with pleasure the joys of the night,
And Mary arose among Friends to be free,
But no Friend from henceforward thou, Mary, shall see.

Some said she was proud, some call'd her a whore,
And some, when she passed by, shut to the door;
A damp cold came o'er her, her blushes all fled;
Her lillies & roses are blighted & shed.

"O, why was I born with a different Face?
Why was I not born like this Envious Race?
Why did Heaven adorn me with bountiful hand,
And then set me down in an envious Land?

"To be weak as a Lamb & smooth as a dove,
And not to raise Envy, is call'd Christian Love;
But if you raise Envy your Merit's to blame
For planting such spite in the weak & the tame.

"I will humble my Beauty, I will not dress fine,
I will keep from the Ball, & my Eyes shall not shine;
And if any Girl's Lover forsakes her for me,
I'll refuse him my hand & from Envy be free."

She went out in Morning attir'd plain & neat;
"Proud Mary's gone Mad," said the Child in the Street;
She went out in Morning in plain neat attire,
And came home in Evening bespatter'd with mire.

She trembled & wept, sitting on the Bed side;
She forgot it was Night, & she trembled & cried;
She forgot it was Night, she forgot it was Morn,
Her soft Memory imprinted with Faces of Scorn.

With Faces of Scorn & with Eyes of disdain
Like foul Fiends inhabiting Mary's mild Brain;
She remembers no Face like the Human Divine.
All Faces have Envy, sweet Mary, but thine;

And thine is a Face of sweet Love in despair,
And thine is a Face of mild sorrow & care,

And thine is a Face of wild terror & fear
That shall never be quiet till laid on its bier.

The Crystal Cabinet

The Maiden caught me in the Wild,
Where I was dancing merrily;
She put me into her Cabinet
And Lock'd me up with a golden Key.

This Cabinet is form'd of Gold
And Pearl & Crystal shining bright,
And within it opens into a World
And a little lovely Moony Night.

Another England there I saw,
Another London with its Tower,
Another Thames & other Hills,
And another pleasant Surrey Bower,

Another Maiden like herself,
Translucent, lovely, shining clear,
Threefold each in the other clos'd—
O, what a pleasant trembling fear!

O, what a smile! a threefold Smile
Fill'd me, that like a flame I burn'd;
I bent to Kiss the lovely Maid,
And found a Threefold Kiss return'd.

I strove to sieze the inmost Form
With ardor fierce & hands of flame,
But burst the Crystal Cabinet,
And like a Weeping Babe became—

A weeping Babe upon the wild,
And Weeping Woman pale reclin'd,

And in the outward air again
I fill'd with woes the passing Wind.

The Grey Monk

"I die, I die!" the Mother said,
"My Children die for lack of Bread.
What more has the merciless Tyrant said?"
The Monk sat down on the Stony Bed.

The blood red ran from the Grey Monk's side,
His hands & feet were wounded wide,
His Body bent, his arms & knees
Like to the roots of ancient trees.

His eye was dry; no tear could flow:
A hollow groan first spoke his woe.
He trembled & shudder'd upon the Bed;
At length with a feeble cry he said:

"When God commanded this hand to write
In the studious hours of deep midnight,
He told me the writing I wrote should prove
The Bane of all that on Earth I lov'd.

"My Brother starv'd between two Walls,
His Children's Cry my Soul appalls;
I mock'd at the wrack & griding chain,
My bent body mocks their torturing pain.

"Thy Father drew his sword in the North,
With his thousands strong he marched forth;
Thy Brother has arm'd himself in Steel
To avenge the wrongs thy Children feel.

"But vain the Sword & vain the Bow,
They never can work War's overthrow.

The Hermit's Prayer & the Widow's tear
Alone can free the World from fear.

"For a Tear is an Intellectual Thing,
And a Sigh is the Sword of an Angel King,
And the bitter groan of the Martyr's woe
Is an Arrow from the Almightie's Bow.

"The hand of Vengeance found the Bed
To which the Purple Tyrant fled;
The iron hand crush'd the Tyrant's head
And became a Tyrant in his stead."

Auguries of Innocence

To see a World in a Grain of Sand
And a Heaven in a Wild Flower,
Hold Infinity in the palm of your hand
And Eternity in an hour.

A Robin Red breast in a Cage
Puts all Heaven in a Rage.
A dove house fill'd with doves & Pigeons
Shudders Hell thro' all its regions.
A dog starv'd at his Master's Gate
Predicts the ruin of the State.
A Horse misus'd upon the Road
Calls to Heaven for Human blood.
Each outcry of the hunted Hare
A fibre from the Brain does tear.
A Skylark wounded in the wing,
A Cherubim does cease to sing.
The Game Cock clip'd & arm'd for fight
Does the Rising Sun affright.
Every Wolf's & Lion's howl
Raises from Hell a Human Soul.
The wild deer, wand'ring here & there,

Keeps the Human Soul from Care.
The Lamb misus'd breeds Public strife
And yet forgives the Butcher's Knife.
The Bat that flits at close of Eve
Has left the Brain that won't Believe.
The Owl that calls upon the Night
Speaks the Unbeliever's fright.
He who shall hurt the little Wren
Shall never be belov'd by Men.
He who the Ox to wrath has mov'd
Shall never be by Woman lov'd.
The wanton Boy that kills the Fly
Shall feel the Spider's enmity.
He who torments the Chafer's sprite
Weaves a Bower in endless Night.
The Catterpiller on the Leaf
Repeats to thee thy Mother's grief.
Kill not the Moth nor Butterfly,
For the Last Judgment draweth nigh.
He who shall train the Horse to War
Shall never pass the Polar Bar.
The Beggar's Dog & Widow's Cat,
Feed them & thou wilt grow fat.
The Gnat that sings his Summer's song
Poison gets from Slander's tongue.
The poison of the Snake & Newt
Is the sweat of Envy's Foot.
The Poison of the Honey Bee
Is the Artist's Jealousy.
The Prince's Robes & Beggar's Rags
Are Toadstools on the Miser's Bags.
A truth that's told with bad intent
Beats all the Lies you can invent.
It is right it should be so;
Man was made for Joy & Woe;
And when this we rightly know
Thro' the World we safely go.

[*Auguries of Innocence*]

Joy & Woe are woven fine,
A Clothing for the Soul divine;
Under every grief & pine
Runs a joy with silken twine.
The Babe is more than swadling Bands;
Throughout all these Human Lands
Tools were made, & Born were hands,
Every Farmer Understands.
Every Tear from Every Eye
Becomes a Babe in Eternity;
This is caught by Females bright
And return'd to its own delight.
The Bleat, the Bark, Bellow & Roar
Are Waves that Beat on Heaven's Shore.
The Babe that weeps the Rod beneath
Writes Revenge in realms of death.
The Beggar's Rags, fluttering in Air,
Does to Rags the Heavens tear.
The Soldier, arm'd with Sword & Gun,
Palsied strikes the Summer's Sun.
The poor Man's Farthing is worth more
Than all the Gold on Afric's Shore.
One Mite wrung from the Labrer's hands
Shall buy & sell the Miser's Lands:
Or, if protected from on high,
Does that whole Nation sell & buy.
He who mocks the Infant's Faith
Shall be mock'd in Age & Death.
He who shall teach the Child to Doubt
The rotting Grave shall ne'er get out.
He who respects the Infant's faith
Triumphs over Hell & Death.
The Child's Toys & the Old Man's Reasons
Are the Fruits of the Two seasons.
The Questioner, who sits so sly,
Shall never know how to Reply.
He who replies to words of Doubt

Doth put the Light of Knowledge out.
The Strongest Poison ever known
Came from Caesar's Laurel Crown.
Nought can deform the Human Race
Like to the Armour's iron brace.
When Gold & Gems adorn the Plow
To peaceful Arts shall Envy Bow.
A Riddle or the Cricket's Cry
Is to Doubt a fit Reply.
The Emmet's Inch & Eagle's Mile
Make Lame Philosophy to smile.
He who Doubts from what he sees
Will ne'er Believe, do what you Please.
If the Sun & Moon should doubt,
They'd immediately Go out.
To be in a Passion you Good may do,
But no Good if a Passion is in you.
The Whore & Gambler, by the State
Licenc'd, build that Nation's Fate.
The Harlot's cry from Street to Street
Shall weave Old England's winding Sheet.
The Winner's Shout, the Loser's Curse,
Dance before dead England's Hearse.
Every Night & every Morn
Some to Misery are Born.
Every Morn & every Night
Some are Born to sweet delight.
Some are Born to sweet delight,
Some are Born to Endless Night.
We are led to Believe a Lie
When we see not Thro' the Eye
Which was Born in a Night to perish in a Night
When the Soul Slept in Beams of Light.
God Appears & God is Light
To those poor Souls who dwell in Night,
But does a Human Form Display
To those who Dwell in Realms of day.

[*Auguries of Innocence*] 102

Long John Brown & Little Mary Bell

Little Mary Bell had a Fairy in a Nut,
Long John Brown had the Devil in his Gut;
Long John Brown lov'd Little Mary Bell,
And the Fairy drew the Devil into the Nut-shell.

Her Fairy Skip'd out & her Fairy Skip'd in;
He laugh'd at the Devil saying 'Love is a Sin.'
The Devil he raged & the Devil he was wroth,
And the Devil enter'd into the Young Man's broth.

He was soon in the Gut of the loving Young Swain,
For John eat & drank to drive away Love's pain;
But all he could do he grew thinner & thinner,
Tho' he eat & drank as much as ten Men for his dinner.

Some said he had a Wolf in his stomach day & night,
Some said he had the Devil & they guess'd right;
The Fairy skip'd about in his Glory, Joy & Pride,
And he laugh'd at the Devil till poor John Brown died.

Then the Fairy skip'd out of the old Nut shell,
And woe & alack for Pretty Mary Bell!
For the Devil crept in when the Fairy skip'd out,
And there goes Miss Bell with her fusty old Nut.

William Bond

I wonder whether the Girls are mad,
And I wonder whether they mean to kill,
And I wonder if William Bond will die,
For assuredly he is very ill.

He went to Church in a May morning
Attended by Fairies, one, two & three;

But the Angels of Providence drove them away,
And he return'd home in Misery.

He went not out to the Field nor Fold,
He went not out to the Village nor Town,
But he came home in a black, black cloud,
And took to his Bed & there lay down.

And an Angel of Providence at his Feet,
And an Angel of Providence at his Head,
And in the midst a Black, Black Cloud,
And in the midst the Sick Man on his Bed.

And on his Right hand was Mary Green,
And on his Left hand was his Sister Jane,
And their tears fell thro' the black, black Cloud
To drive away the sick man's pain.

"O William, if thou dost another Love,
"Dost another Love better than poor Mary,
"Go & take that other to be thy Wife,
"And Mary Green shall her servant be."

"Yes, Mary, I do another Love,
"Another I Love far better than thee,
"And Another I will have for my Wife;
"Then what have I to do with thee?

"For thou art Melancholy Pale,
"And on thy Head is the cold Moon's shine,
"But she is ruddy & bright as day,
"And the sun beams dazzle from her eyne."

Mary trembled & Mary chill'd
And Mary fell down on the right hand floor,
That William Bond & his Sister Jane
Scarce could recover Mary more.

[*William Bond*]

When Mary awoke & found her Laid
On the Right hand of her William dear,
On the Right hand of his loved Bed,
And saw her William Bond so near,

The Fairies that fled from William Bond
Danced around her Shining Head;
They danced over the Pillow white,
And the Angels of Providence left the Bed.

"I thought Love liv'd in the hot sun shine,
But O, he lives in the Moony light!
I thought to find Love in the heat of day,
But sweet Love is the Comforter of Night.

Seek Love in the Pity of others' Woe,
In the gentle relief of another's care,
In the darkness of night & the winter's snow,
In the naked & outcast, Seek Love there!"

The Marriage of Heaven and Hell

THE ARGUMENT

Rintrah roars & shakes his fires in the burden'd air;
Hungry clouds swag on the deep.

Once meek, and in a perilous path,
The just man kept his course along
The vale of death.
Roses are planted where thorns grow,
And on the barren heath
Sing the honey bees.

Then the perilous path was planted,
And a river and a spring

On every cliff and tomb,
And on the bleached bones
Red clay brought forth;

Till the villain left the paths of ease,
To walk in perilous paths, and drive
The just man into barren climes.

Now the sneaking serpent walks
In mild humility,
And the just man rages in the wilds
Where lions roam.

Rintrah roars & shakes his fires in the burden'd air;
Hungry clouds swag on the deep.

As a new heaven is begun, and it is now thirty-three years since its advent, the Eternal Hell revives. And lo! Swedenborg is the Angel sitting at the tomb: his writings are the linen clothes folded up. Now is the dominion of Edom, & the return of Adam into Paradise. See Isaiah xxxiv & xxxv Chap.

Without Contraries is no progression. Attraction and Repulsion, Reason and Energy, Love and Hate, are necessary to Human existence.

From these contraries spring what the religious call Good & Evil. Good is the passive that obeys Reason. Evil is the active springing from Energy.

Good is Heaven. Evil is Hell.

THE VOICE OF THE DEVIL

All Bibles or sacred codes have been the causes of the following Errors:

1. That Man has two real existing principles: Viz: a Body & a Soul.

2. That Energy, call'd Evil, is alone from the Body; & that Reason, call'd Good, is alone from the Soul.

3. That God will torment Man in Eternity for following his Energies.

But the following Contraries to these are True:

1. Man has no Body distinct from his Soul; for that call'd Body is a portion of Soul discern'd by the five Senses, the chief inlets of Soul in this age.

2. Energy is the only life, and is from the Body; and Reason is the bound or outward circumference of Energy.

3. Energy is Eternal Delight.

Those who restrain desire, do so because theirs is weak enough to be restrained; and the restrainer or reason usurps its place & governs the unwilling.

And being restrain'd, it by degrees becomes passive, till it is only the shadow of desire.

The history of this is written in Paradise Lost, & the Governor or Reason is call'd Messiah.

And the original Archangel, or possessor of the command of the heavenly host, is call'd the Devil or Satan, and his children are call'd Sin & Death.

But in the Book of Job, Milton's Messiah is call'd Satan.

For this history has been adopted by both parties.

It indeed appear'd to Reason as if Desire was cast out; but the Devil's account is, that the Messiah fell, & formed a heaven of what he stole from the Abyss.

This is shewn in the Gospel, where he prays to the Father to send the comforter, or Desire, that Reason may have Ideas to build on; the Jehovah of the Bible being no other than he who dwells in flaming fire.

Know that after Christ's death, he became Jehovah.

But in Milton, the Father is Destiny, the Son a Ratio of the five senses, & the Holy-ghost Vacuum!

Note: The reason Milton wrote in fetters when he wrote of Angels & God, and at liberty when of Devils & Hell, is because he was a true Poet and of the Devil's party without knowing it.

A MEMORABLE FANCY

As I was walking among the fires of hell, delighted with the enjoyments of Genius, which to Angels look like torment and insanity, I collected some of their Proverbs; thinking that as the sayings used in a nation mark its character, so the Proverbs of Hell show the nature of Infernal wisdom better than any description of buildings or garments.

When I came home: on the abyss of the five senses, where a flat sided steep frowns over the present world, I saw a mighty Devil folded in black clouds, hovering on the sides of the rock: with corroding fires he wrote the following sentence now percieved by the minds of men, & read by them on earth:

How do you know but ev'ry Bird that cuts the airy way,
Is an immense world of delight, clos'd by your senses five?

PROVERBS OF HELL

In seed time learn, in harvest teach, in winter enjoy.

Drive your cart and your plow over the bones of the dead.

The road of excess leads to the palace of wisdom.

Prudence is a rich, ugly old maid courted by Incapacity.

He who desires but acts not, breeds pestilence.

The cut worm forgives the plow.

Dip him in the river who loves water.

A fool sees not the same tree that a wise man sees.

He whose face gives no light, shall never become a star.

Eternity is in love with the productions of time.

The busy bee has no time for sorrow.

The hours of folly are measur'd by the clock; but of wisdom, no clock can measure.

All wholesome food is caught without a net or a trap.

Bring out number, weight & measure in a year of dearth.

No bird soars too high, if he soars with his own wings.

A dead body revenges not injuries.

The most sublime act is to set another before you.

If the fool would persist in his folly he would become wise.

Folly is the cloke of knavery.

Shame is Pride's cloke.

Prisons are built with stones of Law, Brothels with bricks of Religion.

The pride of the peacock is the glory of God.

The lust of the goat is the bounty of God.

The wrath of the lion is the wisdom of God.

The nakedness of woman is the work of God.

Excess of sorrow laughs. Excess of joy weeps.

The roaring of lions, the howling of wolves, the raging of the stormy sea, and the destructive sword, are portions of eternity, too great for the eye of man.

The fox condemns the trap, not himself.

Joys impregnate. Sorrows bring forth.

Let man wear the fell of the lion, woman the fleece of the sheep.

The bird a nest, the spider a web, man friendship.

The selfish, smiling fool, & the sullen, frowning fool shall be both thought wise, that they may be a rod.

What is now proved was once only imagin'd.

The rat, the mouse, the fox, the rabbet watch the roots; the lion, the tyger, the horse, the elephant watch the fruits.

The cistern contains: the fountain overflows.

One thought fills immensity.

Always be ready to speak your mind, and a base man will avoid you.

Every thing possible to be believ'd is an image of truth.

The eagle never lost so much time as when he submitted to learn of the crow.

The fox provides for himself, but God provides for the lion.

Think in the morning. Act in the noon. Eat in the evening. Sleep in the night.

He who has suffer'd you to impose on him, knows you.

As the plow follows words, so God rewards prayers.

The tygers of wrath are wiser than the horses of instruction.

Expect poison from the standing water.

You never know what is enough unless you know what is more than enough.

Listen to the fool's reproach! it is a kingly title!

The eyes of fire, the nostrils of air, the mouth of water, the beard of earth.

The weak in courage is strong in cunning.

The apple tree never asks the beech how he shall grow; nor the lion, the horse, how he shall take his prey.

The thankful reciever bears a plentiful harvest.

If others had not been foolish, we should be so.

The soul of sweet delight can never be defil'd.

When thou seest an Eagle, thou seest a portion of Genius; lift up thy head!

As the caterpiller chooses the fairest leaves to lay her eggs on, so the priest lays his curse on the fairest joys.

To create a little flower is the labour of ages.

Damn braces. Bless relaxes.

The best wine is the oldest, the best water the newest.

Prayers plow not! Praises reap not!

Joys laugh not! Sorrows weep not!

The head Sublime, the heart Pathos, the genitals Beauty, the hands & feet Proportion.

As the air to a bird or the sea to a fish, so is contempt to the contemptible.

The crow wish'd every thing was black, the owl that every thing was white.

Exuberance is Beauty.

If the lion was advised by the fox, he would be cunning.

Improvement makes strait roads; but the crooked roads without Improvement are roads of Genius.

Sooner murder an infant in its cradle than nurse unacted desires.

Where man is not, nature is barren.

Truth can never be told so as to be understood, and not be believ'd.

Enough! or Too much.

The ancient Poets animated all sensible objects with Gods or Geniuses, calling them by the names and adorning them with the properties of woods, rivers, mountains, lakes, cities, nations, and whatever their enlarged & numerous senses could percieve.

And particularly they studied the genius of each city & country, placing it under its mental deity;

Till a system was formed, which some took advantage of, & enslav'd the vulgar by attempting to realize or abstract the mental deities from their objects: thus began Priesthood;

Choosing forms of worship from poetic tales.

And at length they pronounc'd that the Gods had ordered such things.

Thus men forgot that All deities reside in the human breast.

A MEMORABLE FANCY

The Prophets Isaiah and Ezekiel dined with me, and I asked them how they dared so roundly to assert that God spoke to them; and whether they did not think at the time that they would be misunderstood, & so be the cause of imposition.

Isaiah answer'd: "I saw no God, nor heard any, in a finite organical perception; but my senses discover'd the infinite in everything, and as I was then perswaded, & remain confirm'd, that the voice of honest indignation is the voice of God, I cared not for consequences, but wrote."

Then I asked: "does a firm perswasion that a thing is so, make it so?"

He replied: "All poets believe that it does, & in ages of imagination this firm perswasion removed mountains; but many are not capable of a firm perswasion of any thing."

Then Ezekiel said: "The philosophy of the east taught the first principles of human perception: some nations held one principle for the origin, and some another: we of Israel taught that the Poetic Genius (as you now call it) was the first principle and all the others merely derivative, which was the cause of our despising the Priests & Philosophers of other countries, and prophecying that all Gods would at last be proved to originate in ours & to be the tributaries of the Poetic Genius; it was this that our great poet, King David, desired so fervently & invokes so pathetic'ly, saying by this he conquers enemies & governs kingdoms; and we so loved our God, that we cursed in his name all the deities of surrounding nations, and asserted that they had rebelled: from these opinions the vulgar came to think that all nations would at last be subject to the jews."

"This," said he, "like all firm perswasions, is come to pass; for all nations believe the jews' code and worship the jews' god, and what greater subjection can be?"

I heard this with some wonder, & must confess my own conviction. After dinner I ask'd Isaiah to favour the world with his lost works; he said none of equal value was lost. Ezekiel said the same of his.

I also asked Isaiah what made him go naked and barefoot three years? he answer'd: "the same that made our friend Diogenes, the Grecian."

I then asked Ezekiel why he eat dung, & lay so long on his right & left side? he answer'd, "the desire of raising other men into a perception of the infinite: this the North American tribes practise, & is he honest who resists his genius or conscience only for the sake of present ease or gratification?"

The ancient tradition that the world will be consumed in fire at the end of six thousand years is true, as I have heard from Hell.

For the cherub with his flaming sword is hereby commanded to leave his guard at tree of life; and when he does, the whole creation will be consumed and appear infinite and holy, whereas it now appears finite & corrupt.

This will come to pass by an improvement of sensual enjoyment.

But first the notion that man has a body distinct from his soul is to be expunged; this I shall do by printing in the infernal method, by corrosives, which in Hell are salutary and medicinal, melting apparent surfaces away, and displaying the infinite which was hid.

If the doors of perception were cleansed every thing would appear to man as it is, infinite.

For a man has closed himself up, till he sees all things thro' narrow chinks of his cavern.

A MEMORABLE FANCY

I was in a Printing house in Hell, & saw the method in which knowledge is transmitted from generation to generation.

In the first chamber was a Dragon-Man, clearing away the rubbish from a cave's mouth; within, a number of Dragons were hollowing the cave.

In the second chamber was a Viper folding round the rock & the cave, and others adorning it with gold, silver and precious stones.

In the third chamber was an Eagle with wings and feathers of air: he caused the inside of the cave to be infinite; around were numbers of Eagle-like men who built palaces in the immense cliffs.

In the fourth chamber were Lions of flaming fire, raging around & melting the metals into living fluids.

In the fifth chamber were Unnam'd forms, which cast the metals into the expanse.

There they were reciev'd by Men who occupied the sixth chamber, and took the forms of books & were arranged in libraries.

The Giants who formed this world into its sensual existence, and now seem to live in it in chains, are in truth the causes of its life & the sources of all activity; but the chains are the cunning of weak and tame minds which have power to resist energy; according to the proverb, the weak in courage is strong in cunning.

Thus one portion of being is in the Prolific, the other the Devouring: to the Devourer it seems as if the producer was in his chains; but it is not so, he only takes portions of existence and fancies that the whole.

But the Prolific would cease to be Prolific unless the Devourer, as a sea, received the excess of his delights.

Some will say: "Is not God alone the Prolific?" I answer: "God only Acts & Is, in existing beings or Men."

These two classes of men are always upon earth, & they should be enemies: whoever tries to reconcile them seeks to destroy existence.

Religion is an endeavour to reconcile the two.

Note: Jesus Christ did not wish to unite, but to separate them, as in the Parable of sheep and goats! & he says: "I came not to send Peace, but a Sword."

Messiah or Satan or Tempter was formerly thought to be one of the Antediluvians who are our Energies.

A MEMORABLE FANCY

An Angel came to me and said: "O pitiable foolish young man! O horrible! O dreadful state! consider the hot burning dungeon thou art preparing for thyself to all eternity, to which thou art going in such career."

I said: "Perhaps you will be willing to shew me my eternal lot, & we will contemplate together upon it, and see whether your lot or mine is most desirable."

So he took me thro' a stable & thro' a church & down into the church vault, at the end of which was a mill: thro' the mill we went, and came to a cave: down the winding cavern we groped our tedious way, till a void boundless as a nether sky appear'd beneath us, & we held by the roots of trees and hung over this immensity; but I said: "if you please, we will commit ourselves to this void, and see whether providence is here also: if you will not, I will:" but he answer'd: "do not presume, O young man, but as we here remain, behold thy lot which will soon appear when the darkness passes away."

So I remain'd with him, sitting in the twisted root of an oak; he was suspended in a fungus, which hung with the head downward into the deep.

By degrees we beheld the infinite Abyss, fiery as the smoke of a burning city; beneath us, at an immense distance, was the sun, black but shining; round it were fiery tracks on which revolv'd vast spiders, crawling after their prey, which flew, or rather swum, in the infinite deep, in the most terrific shapes of animals sprung from corruption; & the air was full of them, & seem'd composed of them: these are Devils, and are called Powers of the air. I now asked my companion which was my eternal lot? he said: "between the black & white spiders."

But now, from between the black & white spiders, a cloud and fire burst and rolled thro' the deep, black'ning all beneath, so that the nether deep grew black as a sea, & rolled with a terrible noise; beneath us was nothing now to be seen but a black tempest, till looking east between the clouds & the waves, we saw a cataract of blood mixed with fire, and not many stones' throw from us appear'd and sunk again the scaly fold of a monstrous serpent; at last, to the east, distant about three degrees, appear'd a fiery crest above the waves; slowly it reared like a ridge of golden rocks, till we discover'd two globes of crimson fire, from which the sea fled away in clouds of smoke; and now we saw it was the head of Leviathan; his forehead was divided into streaks of green & purple like those on a tyger's forehead: soon we saw his mouth & red gills hang just above the raging foam, tinging the black deep with beams of blood, advancing toward us with all the fury of a spiritual existence.

My friend the Angel climb'd up from his station into the mill: I remain'd alone; & then this appearance was no more, but I found myself sitting on a pleasant bank beside a river by moonlight, hearing a harper, who sung to the harp; & his theme was: "The man who never alters his opinion is like standing water, & breeds reptiles of the mind."

But I arose and sought for the mill, & there I found my Angel, who, surprised, asked me how I escaped?

I answered: "All that we saw was owing to your metaphysics; for when you ran away, I found myself on a bank by moonlight hearing a harper. But now we have seen my eternal lot, shall I shew you yours?" He laugh'd at my proposal; but I by force suddenly caught him in my arms, & flew westerly thro' the night, till we were elevated above the earth's shadow; then I flung myself with him directly into the body of the sun; here I clothed myself in white, & taking in my hand Swedenborg's volumes, sunk from the glorious clime, and passed all the planets till we came to saturn: here I stay'd to rest, & then leap'd into the void between saturn & the fixed stars.

"Here," said I, "is your lot, in this space—if space it may be call'd." Soon we saw the stable and the church, & I took him to the altar and open'd the Bible, and lo! it was a deep pit, into which I descended, driving the Angel before me; soon we saw seven houses of brick; one we enter'd; in it were a number of monkeys, baboons, & all of that species, chain'd by the middle, grinning and snatching at one another, but withheld by the shortness of their chains: however, I saw that they sometimes grew numerous, and then the weak were caught by the strong, and with a grinning aspect, first coupled with, & then devour'd, by plucking off first one limb and then another, till the body was left a helpless trunk; this, after grinning & kissing it with seeming fondness, they devour'd too; and here & there I saw one savourily picking the flesh off his own tail; as the stench terribly annoy'd us both, we went into the mill, & I in my hand brought the skeleton of a body, which in the mill was Aristotle's Analytics.

So the Angel said: "thy phantasy has imposed upon me, & thou oughtest to be ashamed."

[*The Marriage of Heaven and Hell*] 116

I answer'd: "we impose on one another, & it is but lost time to converse with you whose works are only Analytics."

Opposition is true Friendship. [*Blake may have intended to obliterate this sentence in his manuscript.*]

I have always found that Angels have the vanity to speak of themselves as the only wise; this they do with a confident insolence sprouting from systematic reasoning.

Thus Swedenborg boasts that what he writes is new: tho' it is only the Contents or Index of already publish'd books.

A man carried a monkey about for a shew, & because he was a little wiser than the monkey, grew vain, and conciev'd himself as much wiser than seven men. It is so with Swedenborg: he shews the folly of churches, & exposes hypocrites, till he imagines that all are religious, & himself the single one on earth that ever broke a net.

Now hear a plain fact: Swedenborg has not written one new truth. Now hear another: he has written all the old falsehoods.

And now hear the reason. He conversed with Angels who are all religious, & conversed not with Devils who all hate religion, for he was incapable thro' his conceited notions.

Thus Swedenborg's writings are a recapitulation of all superficial opinions, and an analysis of the more sublime —but no further.

Have now another plain fact. Any man of mechanical talents may, from the writings of Paracelsus or Jacob Behmen, produce ten thousand volumes of equal value with Swedenborg's, and from those of Dante or Shakespear an infinite number.

But when he has done this, let him not say that he knows better than his master, for he only holds a candle in sunshine.

A MEMORABLE FANCY

Once I saw a Devil in a flame of fire, who arose before an Angel that sat on a cloud, and the Devil utter'd these words:

"The worship of God is: Honouring his gifts in other men, each according to his genius, and loving the greatest men best: those who envy or calumniate great men hate God; for there is no other God."

The Angel hearing this became almost blue; but mastering himself he grew yellow, & at last white, pink, & smiling, and then replied:

"Thou Idolater! is not God One? & is not he visible in Jesus Christ? and has not Jesus Christ given his sanction to the law of ten commandments? and are not all other men fools, sinners, & nothings?"

The Devil answer'd: "bray a fool in a morter with wheat, yet shall not his folly be beaten out of him; if Jesus Christ is the greatest man, you ought to love him in the greatest degree; now hear how he has given his sanction to the law of ten commandments: did he not mock at the sabbath and so mock the sabbath's God? murder those who were murder'd because of him? turn away the law from the woman taken in adultery? steal the labor of others to support him? bear false witness when he omitted making a defence before Pilate? covet when he pray'd for his disciples, and when he bid them shake off the dust of their feet against such as refused to lodge them? I tell you, no virtue can exist without breaking these ten commandments. Jesus was all virtue, and acted from impulse, not from rules."

When he had so spoken, I beheld the Angel, who stretched out his arms, embracing the flame of fire, & he was consumed and arose as Elijah.

Note: This Angel, who is now become a Devil, is my particular friend; we often read the Bible together in its infernal or diabolical sense, which the world shall have if they behave well.

[*The Marriage of Heaven and Hell*] 118

I have also The Bible of Hell, which the world shall have whether they will or no.

One Law for the Lion & Ox is Oppression.

A SONG OF LIBERTY

1. The Eternal Female groan'd! it was heard over all the Earth.
2. Albion's coast is sick, silent; the American meadows faint!
3. Shadows of Prophecy shiver along by the lakes and the rivers, and mutter across the ocean: France, rend down thy dungeon!
4. Golden Spain, burst the barriers of old Rome!
5. Cast thy keys, O Rome, into the deep down falling, even to eternity down falling.
6. And weep.
7. In her trembling hand she took the new born terror, howling.
8. On those infinite mountains of light, now barr'd out by the atlantic sea, the new born fire stood before the starry king!
9. Flag'd with grey brow'd snows and thunderous visages, the jealous wings wav'd over the deep.
10. The speary hand burned aloft, unbuckled was the shield, forth went the hand of jealousy among the flaming hair, and hurl'd the new born wonder thro' the starry night.
11. The fire, the fire is falling!
12. Look up! look up! O citizen of London, enlarge thy countenance! O Jew, leave counting gold! return to thy oil and wine. O African! black African! (go, winged thought, widen his forehead.)
13. The fiery limbs, the flaming hair, shot like the sinking sun into the western sea.
14. Wak'd from his eternal sleep, the hoary element roaring fled away.
15. Down rush'd, beating his wings in vain, the jealous

king; his grey brow'd councellors, thunderous warriors, curl'd veterans, among helms, and shields, and chariots, horses, elephants, banners, castles, slings, and rocks.
16. Falling, rushing, ruining! buried in the ruins, on Urthona's dens;
17. All night beneath the ruins; then, their sullen flames faded, emerge round the gloomy king.
18. With thunder and fire, leading his starry hosts thro' the waste wilderness, he promulgates his ten commands, glancing his beamy eyelids over the deep in dark dismay,
19. Where the son of fire in his eastern cloud, while the morning plumes her golden breast,
20. Spurning the clouds written with curses, stamps the stony law to dust, loosing the eternal horses from the dens of night, crying:

EMPIRE IS NO MORE! AND NOW THE LION
& WOLF SHALL CEASE.

CHORUS

Let the Priests of the Raven of dawn no longer, in deadly black, with hoarse note curse the sons of joy. Nor his accepted brethren—whom, tyrant, he calls free—lay the bound or build the roof. Nor pale religious letchery call that virginity that wishes but acts not!

For every thing that lives is Holy.

from *America: A Prophecy*

"The morning comes, the night decays, the watchmen
leave their stations;
The grave is burst, the spices shed, the linen wrapped up;
The bones of death, the cov'ring clay, the sinews shrunk
& dry'd

Reviving shake, inspiring move, breathing, awakening,
Spring like redeemed captives when their bonds & bars are burst.
Let the slave grinding at the mill run out into the field,
Let him look up into the heavens & laugh in the bright air;
Let the inchained soul, shut up in darkness and in sighing,
Whose face has never seen a smile in thirty weary years,
Rise and look out; his chains are loose, his dungeon doors are open;
And let his wife and children return from the oppressor's scourge.
They look behind at every step & believe it is a dream,
Singing: 'The Sun has left his blackness & has found a fresher morning,
And the fair Moon rejoices in the clear & cloudless night;
For Empire is no more, and now the Lion & Wolf shall cease.' "

from *Europe: A Prophecy*

"Five windows light the cavern'd Man: thro' one he breathes the air;
Thro' one hears music of the spheres; thro' one the eternal vine
Flourishes, that he may recieve the grapes; thro' one can look
And see small portions of the eternal world that ever groweth;
Thro' one himself pass out what time he please; but he will not,
For stolen joys are sweet & bread eaten in secret pleasant."

So sang a Fairy, mocking, as he sat on a streak'd Tulip,

Thinking none saw him: when he ceas'd I started from the trees
And caught him in my hat, as boys knock down a butterfly.
"How know you this," said I, "small Sir? where did you learn this song?"
Seeing himself in my possession, thus he answer'd me:
"My master, I am yours! command me, for I must obey."

"Then tell me, what is the material world, and is it dead?"
He, laughing, answer'd: "I will write a book on leaves of flowers,
If you will feed me on love-thoughts & give me now and then
A cup of sparkling poetic fancies; so, when I am tipsie,
I'll sing to you to this soft lute, and shew you all alive
The world, where every particle of dust breathes forth its joy."
I took him home in my warm bosom: as we went along
Wild flowers I gather'd, & he shew'd me each eternal flower:
He laugh'd aloud to see them whimper because they were pluck'd.
They hover'd round me like a cloud of incense: when I came
Into my parlour and sat down and took my pen to write,
My Fairy sat upon the table and dictated EUROPE.

from *Milton*

PREFACE

And did those feet in ancient time
Walk upon England's mountains green?
And was the holy Lamb of God
On England's pleasant pastures seen?

And did the Countenance Divine
Shine forth upon our clouded hills?
And was Jerusalem builded here
Among these dark Satanic Mills?

Bring me my Bow of burning gold:
Bring me my Arrows of desire:
Bring me my Spear: O clouds unfold!
Bring me my Chariot of fire.

I will not cease from Mental Fight,
Nor shall my Sword sleep in my hand
Till we have built Jerusalem
In England's green & pleasant Land.

"Would to God that all the Lord's people were Prophets."
NUMBERS, xi. ch., 29 v.

from *Jerusalem*

The fields from Islington to Marybone,
To Primrose Hill and Saint John's Wood,
Were builded over with pillars of gold,
And there Jerusalem's pillars stood.

Her Little-ones ran on the fields,
The Lamb of God among them seen,
And fair Jerusalem his Bride,
Among the little meadows green.

Pancrass & Kentish-town repose
Among her golden pillars high,
Among her golden arches which
Shine upon the starry sky.

The Jew's-harp-house & the Green Man,
The Ponds where Boys to bathe delight,

The fields of Cows by Willan's farm,
Shine in Jerusalem's pleasant sight.

She walks upon our meadows green,
The Lamb of God walks by her side,
And every English Child is seen
Children of Jesus & his Bride.

Forgiving trespasses and sins
Lest Babylon with cruel Og
With Moral & Self-righteous Law
Should Crucify in Satan's Synagogue!

What are those golden Builders doing
Near mournful ever-weeping Paddington,
Standing above that mighty Ruin
Where Satan the first victory won,

Where Albion slept beneath the Fatal Tree,
And the Druids' golden Knife
Rioted in human gore,
In Offerings of Human Life?

They groan'd aloud on London Stone,
They groan'd aloud on Tyburn's Brook,
Albion gave his deadly groan,
And all the Atlantic Mountains shook.

Albion's Spectre from his Loins
Tore forth in all the pomp of War:
Satan his name: in flames of fire
He stretch'd his Druid Pillars far.

Jerusalem fell from Lambeth's Vale
Down thro' Poplar & Old Bow,
Thro' Malden & across the Sea,
In War & howling, death & woe.

[*from Jerusalem*] 124

The Rhine was red with human blood,
The Danube roll'd a purple tide,
On the Euphrates Satan stood,
And over Asia stretch'd his pride.

He wither'd up sweet Zion's Hill
From every Nation of the Earth;
He wither'd up Jerusalem's Gates,
And in a dark Land gave her birth.

He wither'd up the Human Form
By laws of sacrifice for sin,
Till it became a Mortal Worm,
But O! translucent all within.

The Divine Vision still was seen,
Still was the Human Form Divine,
Weeping in weak & mortal clay,
O Jesus, still the Form was thine.

And thine the Human Face, & thine
The Human Hands & Feet & Breath,
Entering thro' the Gates of Birth
And passing thro' the Gates of Death.

And O thou Lamb of God, whom I
Slew in my dark self-righteous pride,
Art thou return'd to Albion's Land?
And is Jerusalem thy Bride?

Come to my arms & never more
Depart, but dwell for ever here:
Create my Spirit to thy Love:
Subdue my Spectre to thy Fear.

Spectre of Albion! warlike Fiend!
In clouds of blood & ruin roll'd,

I here reclaim thee as my own.
My Selfhood! Satan! arm'd in gold.

Is this thy soft Family-Love,
Thy cruel Patriarchal pride,
Planting thy Family alone,
Destroying all the World beside?

A man's worst enemies are those
Of his own house & family;
And he who makes his law a curse
By his own law shall surely die.

In my Exchanges every Land
Shall walk, & mine in every Land,
Mutual shall build Jerusalem,
Both heart in heart & hand in hand.

◆

I saw a Monk of Charlemaine
Arise before my sight:
I talk'd with the Grey Monk as we stood
In beams of infernal light.

Gibbon arose with a lash of steel,
And Voltaire with a wracking wheel:
The Schools, in clouds of learning roll'd,
Arose with War in iron & gold.

"Thou lazy Monk," they sound afar,
"In vain condemning glorious War;
And in your Cell you shall ever dwell:
Rise, War, & bind him in his Cell!"

The blood red ran from the Grey Monk's side,
His hands & feet were wounded wide,

His body bent, his arms & knees
Like to the roots of ancient trees.

When Satan first the black bow bent
And the Moral Law from the Gospel rent,
He forg'd the Law into a Sword
And spill'd the blood of mercy's Lord.

Titus! Constantine! Charlemaine!
O Voltaire! Rousseau! Gibbon! Vain
Your Grecian Mocks & Roman Sword
Against this image of his Lord!

For a Tear is an Intellectual thing,
And a Sigh is the Sword of an Angel King,
And the bitter groan of a Martyr's woe
Is an Arrow from the Almightie's Bow.

TO THE CHRISTIANS

I give you the end of a golden string,
Only wind it into a ball,
It will lead you in at Heaven's gate
Built in Jerusalem's wall.

from *The Gates of Paradise*

TO THE ACCUSER WHO IS THE GOD OF THIS WORLD

Truly, My Satan, thou art but a Dunce,
And dost not know the Garment from the Man.
Every Harlot was a Virgin once,
Nor can'st thou ever change Kate into Nan.

Tho' thou art Worship'd by the Names Divine
Of Jesus & Jehovah, thou art still
The Son of Morn in weary Night's decline,
The lost Traveller's Dream under the Hill.

An Island in the Moon

In the Moon is a certain Island near by a mighty continent, which small island seems to have some affinity to England, &, what is more extraordinary, the people are so much alike, & their language so much the same, that you would think you was among your friends. In this Island dwells three Philosophers—Suction the Epicurean, Quid the Cynic, & Sipsop the Pythagorean. I call them by the names of those sects, tho' the sects are not ever mention'd there, as being quite out of date; however, the things still remain, and the vanities are the same. The three Philosophers sat together thinking of nothing. In comes Etruscan Column the Antiquarian, & after an abundance of Enquiries to no purpose, sat himself down & described something that nobody listen'd to. So they were employ'd when Mrs. Gimblet came in. The corners of her mouth seem'd—I don't know how, but very odd, as if she hoped you had not an ill opinion of her,—to be sure, we are all poor creatures! Well, she seated [herself] & seem'd to listen with great attention while the Antiquarian seem'd to be talking of virtuous cats. But it was not so; she was thinking of the shape of her eyes & mouth, & he was thinking of his eternal fame. The three Philosophers at this time were each endeavouring to conceal his laughter (not at them but) at his own imagination.

This was the situation of this improving company when, in a great hurry, Inflammable Gass the Wind-finder enter'd. They seem'd to rise & salute each other. Etruscan Column & Inflammable Gass fix'd their eyes on each other; their tongues went in question & answer, but their thoughts were otherwise employ'd. "I don't like his eyes," said Etruscan Column. "He's a foolish puppy," said Inflammable Gass, smiling on him. The 3 Philosophers—the Cynic smiling, the Epicurean seeming studying the flame of the candle, & the Pythagorean playing with the cat—listen'd with open mouths to the edifying discourses.

"Sir," said the Antiquarian, "I have seen these works, & I do affirm that they are no such thing. They seem to me to be the most wretched, paltry, flimsy stuff that ever—"

"What d'ye say? What d'ye say?" said Inflammable Gass. "Why—why, I wish I could see you write so."

"Sir," said the Antiquarian, "according to my opinion the author is an errant blockhead."

"Your reason—Your reason?" said Inflammable Gass. "Why—why, I think it very abominable to call a man a blockhead that you know nothing of."

"Reason, Sir?" said the Antiquarian. "I'll give you an example for your reason. As I was walking along the street I saw a vast number of swallows on the rails of an old Gothic square. They seem'd to be going on their passage, as Pliny says. As I was looking up, a little *outré* fellow, pulling me by the sleeve, cries, 'Pray, Sir, who do all they belong to?' I turn'd myself about with great contempt. Said I, 'Go along, you fool!' 'Fool!' said he, 'who do you call fool? I only ask'd you a civil question.' I had a great mind to have thrash'd the fellow, only he was bigger than I."

Here Etruscan Column left off—Inflammable Gass, recollecting himself [said], "Indeed I do not think the man was a fool, for he seems to me to have been desirous of enquiring into the works of nature!"

"Ha! Ha! Ha!" said the Pythagorean.

It was re-echo'd by Inflammable Gass to overthrow the argument.

Etruscan Column then, starting up & clenching both his fists, was prepared to give a formal answer to the company. But Obtuse Angle, entering the room, having made a gentle bow, proceeded to empty his pockets of a vast number of papers, turned about & sat down, wiped his face with his pocket handkerchief, & shutting his eyes, began to scratch his head.

"Well, gentlemen," said he, "what is the cause of strife?"

The Cynic answer'd, "They are only quarreling about Voltaire."

"Yes," said the Epicurean, "& having a bit of fun with him."

"And," said the Pythagorean, "endeavoring to incorporate their souls with their bodies."

Obtuse Angle, giving a grin, said, "Voltaire understood nothing of the Mathematics, and a man must be a fool i'faith not to understand the Mathematics."

Inflammable Gass, turning round hastily in his chair, said, "Mathematics! He found out a number of Queries in Philosophy."

Obtuse Angle, shutting his eyes & saying that he always understood better when he shut his eyes, [replied], "In the first place, it is of no use for a man to make Queries, but to solve them; for a man may be a fool & make Queries, but a man must have good sound sense to solve them. A query & an answer are as different as a strait line & a crooked one. Secondly—"

"I—I—I—aye! Secondly, Voltaire's a fool," says the Epicurean.

"Pooh!" says the Mathematician, scratching his head with double violence, "It is not worth Quarreling about."

The Antiquarian here got up, &, hemming twice to shew the strength of his Lungs, said, "But, my Good Sir, Voltaire was immersed in matter, & seems to have understood very little but what he saw before his eyes, like the Animal upon the Pythagorean's lap, always playing with its own tail."

"Ha! Ha! Ha!" said Inflammable Gass. "He was the Glory of France. I have got a bottle of air that would spread a Plague."

Here the Antiquarian shrugg'd up his shoulders, & was silent while Inflammable Gass talk'd for half an hour.

When Steelyard, the lawgiver, coming in stalking—with an act of parliament in his hand, said that it was a shameful thing that acts of parliament should be in a free state, it had so engrossed his mind that he did not salute the company.

Mrs. Gimblet drew her mouth downwards.

CHAP 2d

Tilly Lally, the Siptippidist, Aradobo, the Dean of Morocco, Miss Gittipin, Mrs. Nannicantipot, Mrs. Sistagatist, Gibble Gabble, the wife of Inflammable Gass, & Little Scopprell enter'd the room.

(If I have not presented you with every character in the piece, call me Ass.)

CHAP 3d

In the Moon, as Phebus stood over his oriental Gardening, "O ay, come, I'll sing you a song," said the Cynic.

" 'The trumpeter shit in his hat,' " said the Epicurean.

"—& clapt it on his head," said the Pythagorean.

"I'll begin again," said the Cynic.

"Little Phebus came strutting in
With his fat belly & his round chin,
What is it you would please to have?
Ho! Ho!
I won't let it go at only so & so."

Mrs. Gimblet look'd as if they meant her. Tilly Lally laught like a cherry clapper. Aradobo ask'd, "Who was Phebus, Sir?"

Obtuse Angle answer'd quickly, "He was the God of Physic, Painting, Perspective, Geometry, Geography, Astronomy, Cookery, Chymistry, Mechanics, Tactics, Pathology, Phraseology, Theology, Mythology, Astrology, Osteology, Somatology—in short, every art & science adorn'd him as beads round his neck."

Here Aradobo look'd Astonished & ask'd if he understood Engraving.

Obtuse Angle Answer'd, indeed he did.

"Well," said the other, "he was as great as Chatterton."

Tilly Lally turn'd round to Obtuse Angle & ask'd who it was that was as great as Chatterton.

"Hay! How should I know?" Answer'd Obtuse Angle. "Who was It, Aradobo?"

"Why sir," said he, "the Gentleman that the song was about."

"Ah," said Tilly Lally, "I did not hear it. What was it, Obtuse Angle?"

"Pooh," said he. "Nonsense!"

"Mhm," said Tilly Lally.

"It was Phebus," said the Epicurean.

"Ah, that was the Gentleman," said Aradobo.

"Pray, Sir," said Tilly Lally, "who was Phebus?"

Obtuse Angle answer'd, "The heathen in the old ages us'd to have Gods that they worship'd, & they us'd to sacrifice to them. You have read about that in the Bible."

"Ah," said Aradobo, "I thought I had read of Phebus in the Bible."

"Aradobo, you should always think before you speak," said Obtuse Angle.

"Ha! Ha! Ha! He means Pharaoh," said Tilly Lally.

"I am asham'd of you,—making use of the names in the Bible," said Mrs. Sistagatist.

"I'll tell you what, Mrs. Sinagain. I don't think there's any harm in it," said Tilly Lally.

"No," said Inflammable Gass. "I have got a camera obscura at home. What was it you was talking about?"

"Law!" said Tilly Lally. "What has that to do with Pharaoh?"

"Pho! nonsense! hang Pharoh & all his host," said the Pythagorean. "Sing away, Quid."

Then the Cynic sung—

"Honour & Genius is all I ask
And I ask the Gods no more.

"No more, No more,
No more, No more." } the three Philosophers bear Chorus.

Here Aradobo suck'd his under lip.

CHAP 4

"Hang names!" said the Pythagorean, "What's Pharaoh better than Phebus, or Phebus than Pharoh?"

"Hang them both," said the Cynic.

"Don't be prophane," said Mrs. Sistagatist.

"Why?" said Mrs. Nannicantipot, "I don't think it's prophane to say 'Hang Pharoh.' "

"Oh," said Mrs. Sinagain. "I'm sure you ought to hold your tongue, for you never say any thing about the scriptures, & you hinder your husband from going to church."

"Ha, ha!" said Inflammable Gass. "What! don't you like to go to church?"

"No," said Mrs. Nannicantipot. "I think a person may be as good at home."

"If I had not a place of profit that forces me to go to church," said Inflammable Gass, "I'd see the parsons all hang'd,—a parcel of lying—"

"O!" said Mrs. Sistagatist. "If it was not for churches & chapels I should not have liv'd so long. There was I, up in a Morning at four o'clock, when I was a Cirl. I would run like the dickins till I was all in a heat. I would stand till I was ready to sink into the earth. Ah, Mr. Huffcap would kick the bottom of the Pulpit out with Passion—would tear off the sleeve of his Gown & set his wig on fire & throw it at the people. He'd cry & stamp & kick & sweat, and all for the good of their souls."

"I'm sure he must be a wicked villain," said Mrs. Nannicantipot, "a passionate wretch. If I was a man I'd wait at the bottom of the pulpit stairs & knock him down & run away!"

"You would, you Ignorant jade? I wish I could see you

hit any of the ministers! You deserve to have your ears boxed, you do."

"I'm sure this is not religion," answers the other.

Then Mr. Inflammable Gass ran & shov'd his head into the fire & set his hair all in a flame, & ran about the room,—No, no, he did not; I was only making a fool of you.

CHAP 5

Obtuse Angle, Scopprell, Aradobo, & Tilly Lally are all met in Obtuse Angle's study.

"Pray," said Aradobo, "is Chatterton a Mathematician?"

"No," said Obtuse Angle. "How can you be so foolish as to think he was?"

"Oh, I did not think he was—I only ask'd," said Aradobo.

"How could you think he was not, & ask if he was?" said Obtuse Angle.

"Oh no, Sir. I did not think he was, before you told me, but afterwards I thought he was not."

Obtuse Angle said, "In the first place you thought he was, & then afterwards when I said he was not, you thought he was not. Why, I know that—"

"Oh no, sir, I thought that he was not, but I ask'd to know whether he was."

"How can that be?" said Obtuse Angle. "How could you ask & think that he was not?"

"Why," said he, "it came into my head that he was not."

"Why then," said Obtuse Angle, "you said that he was."

"Did I say so? Law! I did not think I said that."

"Did not he?" said Obtuse Angle.

"Yes," said Scopprell.

"But I meant—" said Aradobo, "I—I—I can't think. Law! Sir, I wish you'd tell me how it is."

Then Obtuse Angle put his chin in his hand & said,

"Whenever you think, you must always think for yourself."

"How, sir?" said Aradobo. "Whenever I think, I must think myself? I think I do. In the first place—" said he with a grin.

"Poo! Poo!" said Obtuse Angle. "Don't be a fool."

Then Tilly Lally took up a Quadrant & ask'd, "Is not this a sun-dial?"

"Yes," said Scopprell, "but it's broke."

At this moment the three Philosophers enter'd, and low'ring darkness hover'd over the assembly.

"Come," said the Epicurean, "let's have some rum & water, & hang the mathematics! Come, Aradobo! Say some thing."

Then Aradobo began, "In the first place I think, I think in the first place that Chatterton was clever at Fissic, Follogy, Pistinology, Aridology, Arography, Transmography, Phizography, Hogamy, Hatomy, & hall that, but, in the first place, he eat wery little, wickly—that is, he slept very little, which he brought into a consumsion; & what was that that he took? Fissic or somethink,—& so died!"

So all the people in the book enter'd into the room, & they could not talk any more to the present purpose.

CHAP 6

They all went home & left the Philosophers. Then Suction Ask'd if Pindar was not a better Poet than Ghiotto was a Painter.

"Plutarch has not the life of Ghiotto," said Sipsop.

"No," said Quid, "to be sure, he was an Italian."

"Well," said Suction, "that is not any proof."

"Plutarch was a nasty ignorant puppy," said Quid. "I hate your sneaking rascals. There's Aradobo in ten or twelve years will be a far superior genius."

"Ah!" said the Pythagorean, "Aradobo will make a very clever fellow."

"Why," said Quid, "I think that any natural fool would make a clever fellow, if he was properly brought up."

"Ah, hang your reasoning!" said the Epicurean. "I hate reasoning. I do everything by my feelings."

"Ah!" said Sipsop, "I only wish Jack Tearguts had had the cutting of Plutarch. He understands Anatomy better than any of the Ancients. He'll plunge his knife up to the hilt in a single drive and thrust his fist in, and all in the space of a Quarter of an hour. He does not mind their crying, tho' they cry ever so. He'll swear at them & keep them down with his fist, & tell them that he'll scrape their bones if they don't lay still & be quiet. What the devil should the people in the hospital that have it done for nothing make such a piece of work for?"

"Hang that," said Suction; "let us have a song."

Then the Cynic sang—

1.

"When old corruption first begun,
  Adorn'd in yellow vest,
He committed on flesh a whoredom—
  O, what a wicked beast!

2.

"From then a callow babe did spring,
  And old corruption smil'd
To think his race should never end,
  For now he had a child.

3.

"He call'd him surgery, & fed
  The babe with his own milk,
For flesh & he could ne'er agree,
  She would not let him suck.

4.

"And this he always kept in mind,

And form'd a crooked knife,
And ran about with bloody hands
To seek his mother's life.

5.

"And as he ran to seek his mother
He met with a dead woman,
He fell in love & married her,
A deed which is not common.

6.

"She soon grew pregnant & brought forth
Scurvy & spott'd fever.
The father grin'd & skipt about,
And said, 'I'm made for ever!

7.

" 'For now I have procur'd these imps
I'll try experiments.'
With that he tied poor scurvy down
& stopt up all its vents.

8.

"And when the child began to swell,
He shouted out aloud,
'I've found the dropsy out, & soon
Shall do the world more good.'

9.

"He took up fever by the neck
And cut out all its spots,
And thro' the holes which he had made
He first discover'd guts."

"Ah," said Sipsop, "you think we are rascals—& we think you are rascals. I do as I chuse. What is it to any body what I do? I am always unhappy too. When I think of Surgery—I don't know. I do it because I like it. My father does what he likes & so do I. I think, somehow, I'll leave it off. There was a woman having her cancer cut, & she shriek'd so that I was quite sick."

"Good-night," said Sipsop.

CHAP 7

"Good-night," said the other two.

Then Quid & Suction were left alone. Then said Quid, "I think that Homer is bombast, & Shakespeare is too wild, & Milton has no feelings: they might be easily outdone. Chatterton never writ those poems! A parcel of fools, going to Bristol! If I was to go, I'd find it out in a minute, but I've found it out already."

"If I don't knock them all up next year in the Exhibition, I'll be hang'd," said Suction. "Hang Philosophy! I would not give a farthing for it! Do all by your feelings, and never think at all about it. I'm hang'd if I don't get up to-morrow morning by four o'clock & work Sir Joshua."

"Before ten years are at an end," said Quid, "how I will work those poor milksop devils,—an ignorant pack of wretches!"

So they went to bed.

CHAP 8

Steelyard the Lawgiver, sitting at his table, taking extracts from Hervey's Meditations among the tombs & Young's Night thoughts.

"He is not able to hurt me," said he, "more than making me Constable or taking away the parish business. Hah!

" 'My crop of corn is but a field of tares',

says Jerome. Happiness is not for us, poor crawling reptiles of the earth. Talk of happiness & happiness! It's no such thing. Every person has a something.

"Hear then the pride & knowledge of a Sailor,
His sprit sail, fore sail, main sail, & his mizen.
A poor frail man! God wot, I know none frailer.
I know no greater sinner than John Taylor.

If I had only myself to care for I'd soon make Double Elephant look foolish, & Filligreework. I hope [I] shall live to see—

" 'The wreck of matter & the crush of worlds',

as Young says."

Obtuse Angle enter'd the Room.

"What news, Mr. Steelyard?"

"I am reading Thison & Aspasio," said he.

Obtuse Angle took up the books one by one.

"I don't find it here," said he.

"O no," said the other, "it was the meditations!"

Obtuse Angle took up the book & read till the other was quite tir'd out.

Then Scopprell & Miss Gittipin coming in, Scopprell took up a book & read the following passage:—

"An Easy of Huming Understanding, by John Lookye Gent."

"John Locke," said Obtuse Angle.

"O, ay—Lock," said Scopprell.

"Now here," said Miss Gittipin,—"I never saw such company in my life. You are always talking of your books. I like to be where we talk. You had better take a walk, that we may have some pleasure. I am sure I never see any pleasure. There's Double Elephant's Girls, they have their own way; & there's Miss Filligreework, she goes out in her coaches, & her footman & her maids, & Stormonts & Balloon hats, & a pair of Gloves every day, & the Sorrows of Werter, & Robinsons, & the Queen of France's Puss colour, & my Cousin Gibble Gabble says that I am like nobody else. I might as well be in a nunnery. There they go in Postchaises & Stages to Vauxhall

& Ranelagh. And I hardly know what a coach is, except when I go to Mr. Jacko's. He knows what riding is, & his wife is the most agreeable woman. You hardly know she has a tongue in her head, and he is the funniest fellow, & I do believe he'll go in partnership with his master, & they have black servants lodge at their house. I never saw such a place in my life. He says he has six & twenty rooms in his house, and I believe it, & he is not such a liar as Quid thinks he is."

"Poo! Poo! Hold your tongue. Hold your tongue," said the Lawgiver.

This quite provok'd Miss Gittipin, to interrupt her in her favourite topic, & she proceeded to use every Provoking speech that ever she could, & he bore it more like a Saint than a Lawgiver, and with great solemnity he address'd the company in these words:—

"They call women the weakest vessel, but I think they are the strongest. A girl has always more tongue than a boy. I have seen a little brat no higher than a nettle, & she had as much tongue as a city clark; but a boy would be such a fool, not have any thing to say, and if anybody ask'd him a question he would put his head into a hole & hide it. I am sure I take but little pleasure. You have as much pleasure as I have. There I stand & bear every fool's insult. If I had only myself to care for, I'd wring off their noses."

To this Scopprell answer'd, "I think the Ladies' discourses, Mr. Steelyard, are some of them more improving than any book. That is the way I have got some of my knowledge."

"Then," said Miss Gittipin, "Mr. Scopprell, do you know the song of Phebe and Jellicoe?"

"No, Miss," said Scopprell.

Then she repeated these verses, while Steelyard walk'd about the room:

"Phebe, dressed like beautie's Queen,
Jellicoe in faint pea green,

Sitting all beneath a grot
Where the little lambkins trot;

"Maidens dancing, loves a-sporting,
All the country folks a-courting,
Susan, Johnny, Bet, & Joe
Lightly tripping on a row.

"Happy people, who can be
In happiness compar'd with ye?
The Pilgrim with his crook & hat
Sees your happiness compleat."

"A charming song, indeed, Miss," said Scopprell. Here they receiv'd a summons for a merry making at the Philosopher's house.

CHAP 9

"I say, this evening we'll get drunk—I say—dash!—an Anthem, an Anthem!" said Suction.

"Lo the Bat with Leathern wing,
Winking & blinking,
Winking & blinking,
Winking & blinking,
Like Doctor Johnson."

Quid.
" 'Oho', said Dr. Johnson
To Scipio Africanus,
'If you don't own me a Philosopher,
I'll kick your Roman Anus'."

Suction.
" 'Aha', To Dr. Johnson
Said Scipio Africanus,

'Lift up my Roman Petticoat
And kiss my Roman Anus'."

"And the Cellar goes down with a step."
(Grand Chorus).

"Ho, Ho, Ho, Ho, Ho, Ho, Ho, Hooooo, my poooooor siiides! I, I should die if I was to live here!" said Scopprell. "Ho, Ho, Ho, Ho, Ho!"

1st *Vo.* "Want Matches?"
2nd *Vo.* "Yes, yes, yes."
1st *Vo.* "Want Matches?"
2nd *Vo.* "No."

1st *Vo.* "Want Matches?"
2nd *Vo.* "Yes, yes, yes."
1st *Vo.* "Want Matches?"
2nd *Vo.* "No."

Here was great confusion & disorder. Aradobo said that the boys in the street sing something very pretty & funny about London—O no, about Matches. Then Mrs. Nannicantipot sung:

"I cry my matches as far as Guild hall;
God bless the duke & his aldermen all!"

Then sung Scopprell:

"I ask the Gods no more,—
no more, no more."

"Then," said Suction, "come, Mr. Lawgiver, your song"; and the Lawgiver sung:

"As I walk'd forth one may morning

To see the fields so pleasant & so gay,
O there did I spy a young maiden sweet,
Among the Violets that smell so sweet,
    Smell so sweet,
    Smell so sweet,
Among the Violets that smell so sweet."

"Hang your Violets! Here's your Rum & water. O ay," said Tilly Lally, "Joe Bradley & I was going along one day in the sugar-house. Joe Bradley saw—for he had but one eye—saw a treacle Jar. So he goes of his blind side & dips his hand up to the shoulder in treacle. 'Here, lick, lick, lick, lick!' said he. Ha! Ha! Ha! Ha! For he had but one eye. Ha! Ha! Ha! Ho!"

Then sung Scopprell:

"And I ask the Gods no more,—
    no more, no more,
    no more, no more.

"Miss Gittipin," said he, "you sing like a harpsichord. Let your bounty descend to our fair ears and favour us with a fine song."

Then she sung:

"This frog he would a-wooing ride,
  Kitty alone—Kitty alone,—
This frog he would a-wooing ride,—
  Kitty alone & I!
Sing cock I cary, Kitty alone,
  Kitty alone,—Kitty alone,—
Cock I cary, Kitty alone,—
  Kitty alone & I!"

"Charming! Truly elegant!" said Scopprell.

"And I ask the gods no more!"

"Hang your serious songs!" said Sipsop, & he sung as follows: —

"Fa ra so bo ro
  Fa ra bo ra
Sa ba ra ra ba rare roro
Sa ra ra ra bo ro ro ro
  Radara
Sarapodo no flo ro."

"Hang Italian songs! Let's have English!" said Quid. "English genius for ever! Here I go:

"Hail Matrimony, made of Love,
To thy wide gates how great a drove
  On purpose to be yok'd do come!
Widows & maids & youths also,
That lightly trip on beauty's toe,
  Or sit on beauty's bum.

"Hail, finger-footed lovely Creatures!
The females of our human Natures,
  Formed to suckle all Mankind.
'Tis you that come in time of need;
Without you we should never Breed,
  Or any Comfort find.

"For if a Damsel's blind or lame,
Or Nature's hand has crooked her frame,
  Or if she's deaf, or is wall eyed,
Yet if her heart is well inclined,
Some tender lover she shall find
  That panteth for a Bride.

"The universal Poultice this,
To cure whatever is amiss
  In damsel or in widow gay.
It makes them smile, it makes them skip,

Like Birds just cured of the pip,
  They chirp, & hop away.

"Then come ye maidens, come ye swains,
Come & be cured of all your pains
  In Matrimony's Golden cage."

"Go & be hanged!" said Scopprell. "How can you have the face to make game of matrimony?"

Then Quid call'd upon Obtuse Angle for a Song, & he, wiping his face & looking on the corner of the ceiling, sang:

"To be, or not to be
Of great capacity,
  Like Sir Isaac Newton,
Or Locke, or Doctor South,
Or Sherlock upon death?
  I'd rather be Sutton.

"For he did build a house
For aged men & youth,
  With walls of brick & stone.
He furnish'd it within
With whatever he could win,
  And all his own.

"He drew out of the Stocks
His money in a box,
  And sent his servant
To Green the Bricklayer
And to the Carpenter:
  He was so fervent.

"The chimneys were three score,
The windows many more,
  And for convenience
He sinks & gutters made

And all the way he pav'd
  To hinder pestilence.

"Was not this a good man,
Whose life was but a span,
  Whose name was Sutton,—
As Locke, or Doctor South,
Or Sherlock upon Death,
  Or Sir Isaac Newton?"

The Lawgiver was very attentive & beg'd to have it sung over again & again, till the company were tired & insisted on the Lawgiver singing a song himself, which he readily complied with.

"This city & this country has brought forth many mayors,
To sit in state & give forth laws out of their old oak chairs,
With face as brown as any nut with drinking of strong ale;
Good English hospitality, O then it did not fail!

"With scarlet gowns & broad gold lace would make a yeoman sweat,
With stockings roll'd above their knees & shoes as black as jet,
With eating beef & drinking beer, O they were stout & hale!
Good English hospitality, O then it did not fail!

"Thus sitting at the table wide, the Mayor & Aldermen
Were fit to give law to the city; each eat as much as ten.
The hungry poor enter'd the hall, to eat good beef & ale.
Good English hospitality, O then it did not fail!"

Here they gave a shout, & the company broke up.

[*An Island in the Moon*]

CHAP 10

Thus these happy Islanders spent their time. But felicity does not last long, for being met at the house of Inflammable Gass the windfinder, the following affairs happen'd.

"Come, Flammable," said Gibble Gabble, "& let's enjoy ourselves. Bring the Puppets."

"Hay,—Hay," said he, "you—sho—why—ya, ya. How can you be so foolish? Ha! Ha! Ha! She calls the experiments puppets!"

Then he went up stairs & loaded the maid with glasses, & brass tubes, & magic pictures.

"Here, ladies & gentlemen," said he, "I'll shew you a louse, or a flea, or a butterfly, or a cockchafer, the blade bone of a tittleback. No, no. Here's a bottle of wind that I took up in the boghouse, and—O dear, O dear, the water's got into the sliders! Look here, Gibble Gabble! Lend me your handkerchief, Tilly Lally."

Tilly Lally took out his handkerchief, which smear'd the glass worse than ever. Then he screw'd it on. Then he took the sliders, & then he set up the glasses for the Ladies to view the pictures. Thus he was employ'd, & quite out of breath. While Tilly Lally & Scopprell were pumping at the air-pump, Smack went the glass.

"Hang!" said Tilly Lally.

Inflammable Gass turn'd short round & threw down the table & Glasses, & Pictures, & broke the bottles of wind, & let out the Pestilence. He saw the Pestilence fly out of the bottle, & cried out, while he ran out of the room:

"Come out! Come out! We are putrified! We are corrupted! Our lungs are destroy'd with the Flogiston. This will spread a plague all thro' the Island!"

He was downstairs the very first. On the back of him came all the others in a heap.

So they need not bidding go.

CHAP II

Another merry meeting at the house of Steelyard the Lawgiver. After supper, Steelyard & Obtuse Angle had pump'd Inflammable Gass quite dry. They play'd at forfeits, & try'd every method to get good humour.

Said Miss Gittipin, "Pray, Mr. Obtuse Angle, sing us a song."

Then he sung:

"Upon a holy thursday, their innocent faces clean,
The children walking two & two in grey & blue & green,
Grey headed beadles walk'd before with wands as white as snow,
Till into the high dome of Paul's they like thames' waters flow.

"O what a multitude they seem'd, these flowers of London town!
Seated in companies, they sit with radiance all their own.
The hum of multitudes were there, but multitudes of lambs,
Thousands of little girls & boys raising their innocent hands.

"Then like a mighty wind they raise to heav'n the voice of song,
Or like harmonious thunderings the seats of heav'n among.
Beneath them sit the rev'rend men, the guardians of the poor;
Then cherish pity lest you drive an angel from your door."

After this they all sat silent for a quarter of an hour, & Mrs. Nannicantipot said, "It puts me in Mind of my mother's song,

"When the tongues of children are heard on the green,
And laughing is heard on the hill,
My heart is at rest within my breast,
And every thing else is still.

" 'Then come home, my children, the sun is gone down,
And the dews of night arise;
Come, Come, leave off play, & let us away
Till the morning appears in the skies.'

" 'No, No, let us play, for it is yet day,
And we cannot go to sleep
Besides in the sky the little birds fly,
And the meadows are cover'd with sheep.'

" 'Well, Well, go & play till the light fades away,
And then go home to bed.'
The little ones leaped, & shouted, & laugh'd,
And all the hills ecchoed."

Then sung Quid:

"O father, father, where are you going?
Oh do not walk so fast;
Oh, speak, father, speak to your little boy,
Or else I shall be lost.

"The night it was dark & no father was there,
And the child was wet with dew.
The mire was deep, & the child did weep,
And away the vapour flew."

Here nobody could sing any longer, till Tilly Lally pluck'd up a spirit & he sung:

"I say, you Joe,
Throw us the ball.

I've a good mind to go,
And leave you all.

"I never saw such a bowler,
To bowl the ball in a tansey,
And to clean it with my hankercher
Without saying a word.

"That Bill's a foolish fellow,
He has given me a black eye.
He does not know how to handle a bat
Any more than a dog or a cat.

"He has knock'd down the wicket
And broke the stumps,
And runs without shoes to save his pumps."

Here a laugh began, and Miss Gittipin sung:

"Leave, O leave me to my sorrows,
Here I'll sit & fade away;
Till I'm nothing but a spirit,
And I lose this form of clay.

"Then if chance along this forest
Any walk in pathless ways,
Thro' the gloom he'll see my shadow,
Hear my voice upon the Breeze."

The Lawgiver all the while sat delighted to see them in such a serious humour. "Mr. Scopprell," said he, "you must be acquainted with a great many songs."

"Oh, dear sir! Ho, Ho, Ho, I am no singer. I must beg of one of these tender-hearted ladies to sing for me."

They all declined, & he was forced to sing himself:

"There's Dr. Clash
And Signior Falalasole:

O they sweep in the cash
  Into their purse hole.
    Fa me la sol, La me fa sol.

"Great A, little A,
  Bouncing B.
Play away, Play away,
  You're out of the key.
    Fa me la sol, La me fa sol.

"Musicians should have
  A pair of very good ears,
And Long fingers & thumbs,
  And not like clumsy bears.
    Fa me la sol, La me fa sol.

"Gentlemen, Gentlemen!
  Rap, rap, rap,
Fiddle, Fiddle, Fiddle,
  Clap, Clap, Clap.
    Fa me la sol, La me fa sol."

"Hm," said the Lawgiver, "Funny enough. Let's have Handel's water piece." Then Sipsop sung:

"A crowned king,
On a white horse sitting,
With his trumpets sounding,
And Banners flying,
Thro' the clouds of smoke he makes his way,
And the shout of his thousands fills his heart with rejoicing & victory:
And the shout of his thousands fills his heart with rejoicing & victory.
Victory! Victory! 'twas William, the prince of Orange,—

[*A leaf, at least, of the manuscript is missing*]

"—thus Illuminating the Manuscript."

"Ay," said she, "that would be excellent."

"Then," said he, "I would have all the writing Engraved instead of Printed, & at every other leaf a high finish'd print—all in three Volumes folio—& sell them a hundred pounds apiece. They would print off two thousand."

"Then," said she, "whoever will not have them will be ignorant fools & will not deserve to live."

"Don't you think I have something of the Goat's face?" says he.

"Very like a Goat's face," she answer'd.

"I think your face," said he, "is like that noble beast the Tyger. Oh, I was at Mrs. Sicknacker's, & I was speaking of my abilities, but their nasty hearts, poor devils, are eat up with envy. They envy me my abilities, & all the women envy your abilities."

"My dear, they hate people who are of higher abilities than their nasty, filthy selves. But do you outface them, & then strangers will see that you have an opinion."

"Now I think we should do as much good as we can when we are at Mr. Femality's. Do you snap, & take me up, and I will fall into such a passion. I'll hollow and stamp, & frighten all the People there, & show them what truth is."

At this Instant Obtuse Angle came in.

"Oh, I am glad you are come," said Quid.

Poems from *Letters*

To my Dearest Friend, John Flaxman . . .

I bless thee, O Father of Heaven & Earth, that ever I saw
 Flaxman's face.
Angels stand round my Spirit in Heaven, the blessed of
 Heaven are my friends upon Earth.
When Flaxman was taken to Italy, Fuseli was given to
 me for a season,

And now Flaxman hath given me Hayley his friend to be mine, such my lot upon Earth.
Now my lot in the Heavens is this, Milton lov'd me in childhood & shew'd me his face.
Ezra came with Isaiah the Prophet, but Shakespeare in riper years gave me his hand;
Paracelsus & Behmen appear'd to me, terrors appear'd in the Heavens above
And in Hell beneath, & a mighty & awful change threatened the Earth.
The American War began. All its dark horrors passed before my face
Across the Atlantic to France. Then the French Revolution commenc'd in thick clouds,
And My Angels have told me that seeing such visions I could not subsist on the Earth,
But by my conjunction with Flaxman, who knows to forgive Nervous Fear.

To Mrs. Butts

Wife of the Friend of those I most revere,
Recieve this tribute from a Harp sincere;
Go on in Virtuous Seed sowing on Mold
Of Human Vegetation, & Behold
Your Harvest Springing to Eternal Life,
Parent of Youthful Minds, & happy Wife!

◆

With happiness stretch'd across the hills
In a cloud that dewy sweetness distills,
With a blue sky spread over with wings
And a mild sun that mounts & sings,
With trees & fields full of Fairy elves
And little devils who fight for themselves—

Rememb'ring the Verses that Hayley sung
When my heart knock'd against the root of my tongue—
With Angels planted in Hawthorn bowers
And God himself in the passing hours,
With Silver Angels across my way
And Golden Demons that none can stay,
With my Father hovering upon the wind
And my Brother Robert just behind
And my Brother John, the evil one,
In a black cloud making his mone;
Tho' dead, they appear upon my path,
Notwithstanding my terrible wrath:
They beg, they intreat, they drop their tears,
Fill'd full of hopes, fill'd full of fears—
With a thousand Angels upon the Wind
Pouring disconsolate from behind
To drive them off, & before my way
A frowning Thistle implores my stay.
What to others a trifle appears
Fills me full of smiles or tears;
For double the vision my Eyes do see,
And a double vision is always with me.
With my inward Eye 'tis an old Man grey;
With my outward, a Thistle across my way.

"If thou goest back," the thistle said,
"Thou art to endless woe betray'd;
For here does Theotormon lower
And here is Enitharmon's bower
And Los the terrible thus hath sworn,
Because thou backward dost return,
Poverty, Envy, old age & fear
Shall bring thy Wife upon a bier;
And Butts shall give what Fuseli gave,
A dark black Rock & a gloomy Cave."

I struck the Thistle with my foot,
And broke him up from his delving root:

"Must the duties of life each other cross?
Must every joy be dung & dross?
Must my dear Butts feel cold neglect
Because I give Hayley his due respect?
Must Flaxman look upon me as wild,
And all my friends be with doubts beguil'd?
Must my Wife live in my Sister's bane,
Or my Sister survive on my Love's pain?
The curses of Los, the terrible shade,
And his dismal terrors make me afraid."

So I spoke & struck in my wrath
The old man weltering upon my path.
Then Los appear'd in all his power:
In the Sun he appear'd, descending before
My face in fierce flames; in my double sight
'Twas outward a Sun, inward Los in his might.

"My hands are labour'd day & night,
And Ease comes never in my sight.
My Wife has no indulgence given
Except what comes to her from heaven.
We eat little, we drink less;
This Earth breeds not our happiness.
Another Sun feeds our life's streams,
We are not warmed with thy beams;
Thou measurest not the Time to me,
Nor yet the Space that I do see;
My Mind is not with thy light array'd,
Thy terrors shall not make me afraid."
When I had my Defiance given,
The Sun stood trembling in heaven;
The Moon that glow'd remote below,
Became leprous & white as snow;
And every soul of men on the Earth
Felt affliction & sorrow & sickness & dearth.
Los flam'd in my path, & the Sun was hot

With the bows of my Mind & the Arrows of Thought—
My bowstring fierce with Ardour breathes,
My arrows glow in their golden sheaves;
My brother & father march before;
The heavens drop with human gore.

Now I a fourfold vision see,
And a fourfold vision is given to me;
'Tis fourfold in my supreme delight
And threefold in soft Beulah's night
And twofold Always. May God us keep
From Single vision & Newton's sleep!

◆

O why was I born with a different face?
Why was I not born like the rest of my race?
When I look each one starts! when I speak, I offend;
Then I'm silent & passive & lose every Friend.

Then my verse I dishonour, My pictures despise,
My person degrade & my temper chastise;
And the pen is my terror, the pencil my shame;
All my Talents I bury, and dead is my Fame.

I am either too low or too highly priz'd;
When Elate I am Envy'd, When Meek I'm despis'd.

Notes

POETICAL SKETCHES: a long and careful study of this book was prepared by Margaret Ruth Lowery, *Windows of the Morning*, 1940. For reasons of space several rhetorical prose poems have been omitted. These were early attempts at "prophetical" writing.

POEMS WRITTEN IN A COPY OF POETICAL SKETCHES. These were written on the flyleaves of a copy belonging to Nancy Flaxman.

SONG 2ND BY A YOUNG SHEPHERD is a presumably earlier version of the "Laughing Song" in *Songs of Innocence*.

SONGS OF INNOCENCE were engraved in 1789, and drafts of some of them can be found in *An Island in the Moon*, c.1784.

SONGS OF EXPERIENCE were engraved in 1794 and a title for both works was later added. A comparison of the same and contrasting titles shows how Blake envisaged them as a single work.

THE ROSSETTI MS once belonged to Dante Gabriel Rossetti, and had been Blake's younger brother Robert's sketch book before he took it to use as a notebook from about 1793–1811. It has been edited and reproduced in facsimile by Geoffrey Keynes, *The Notebook of William Blake*, 1934.

I ASKED A THIEF TO STEAL ME A PEACH: the version given here was one transcribed as a fair copy from the Notebook and consequently seeming to give Blake's final intention for the poem.

TO THE QUEEN is not from the Rossetti MS, but was written about 1807 and was offered with a design to be engraved to R. H. Cromek to form the dedication to Blair's *The Grave*. The offer of the design, for four guineas, called forth a vitriolic letter from Cromek, printed in Gilchrist's *Life*.

THE PICKERING MS, which takes its name from Mr. B. M. Pickering who bought it in 1866, dates from the Felpham period of 1800–1803, and consists of fair copies of poems.

THE MARRIAGE OF HEAVEN AND HELL is not dated, but the reference to "thirty-three years" makes it certain that it was written in 1790, as that was the period from Blake's birth and Swedenborg's statement that the Last Judgment had occurred in the spirit world in 1757.

AMERICA: A PROPHECY was etched on 18 plates in 1793.

EUROPE: A PROPHECY was etched on 18 plates in 1794.

MILTON. The copy purchased by Thomas Griffith Wainwright, artist and poisoner, contains fifty plates and is on paper watermarked 1815.

JERUSALEM consists of 100 plates. The watermarks show that the printing of none of the known copies can have begun before 1818 or been finished before 1820.

THE GATES OF PARADISE consists of a series of designs etched in 1793 and then reissued with a text in 1818.

AN ISLAND IN THE MOON has been supplied with a title taken from the first line of the satire which was probably written about 1784–1785. It is probable that the satire is aimed not only at the circle surrounding the Rev. Anthony Stephen Matthews but also at the Lunar Society connected with Thomas Taylor, the Platonist, Dr. Joseph Priestley, Erasmus Darwin, Charlotte Lennox, Josiah Wedgwood and others.

POEMS FROM LETTERS

TO MY DEAREST FRIEND, JOHN FLAXMAN: Letter to Flaxman from Lambeth, September 12, 1800.

TO MRS. BUTTS: from the same.

WITH HAPPINESS STRETCH'D: Letter to Butts from Felpham, November 22, 1802.

O WHY WAS I BORN WITH A DIFFERENT FACE: Letter to Butts from Felpham, August 16, 1803.

THE LAUREL POETRY SERIES

General Editor, Richard Wilbur

The Laurel Poetry Series now includes the finest works of British and American poets, as selected by outstanding critics and poets. In addition, each volume contains an original introduction, a chronology of the poet's career, a bibliography, and notes on the poetry.

BLAKE Edited by Ruthven Todd 159 pages/40c
BROWNING Edited by Reed Whitmore 160 pages/40c
BYRON Edited by George R. Creeger 192 pages/40c
CHAUCER Edited by Louis O. Coxe 352 pages/75c
COLERIDGE Edited by G. Robert Stange 159 pages/40c
EMILY DICKINSON Edited by John Malcolm Brinnin 160 pages/40c
DONNE Edited by Andrew Wanning 192 pages/40c
DRYDEN Edited by Reuben Brower 160 pages/35c
HERBERT Edited by Dudley Fitts 191 pages/35c
HERRICK Edited by William Jay Smith 160 pages/40c
JONSON Edited by John Hollander 160 pages/40c
KEATS Edited by Howard Moss 160 pages/40c
LONGFELLOW Edited by Howard Nemerov 160 pages/35c
MARVELL Edited by Joseph H. Summers 160 pages/35c
MILTON Edited by William G. Madsen 190 pages/35c
POE Edited by Richard Wilbur 160 pages/40c
POPE Edited by John Wain 157 pages/40c
SHELLEY Edited by William Meredith 191 pages/40c
SPENSER Edited by Edwin Honig 368 pages/75c
WHITMAN Edited by Leslie A. Fiedler 192 pages/40c
WHITTIER Edited by Donald Hall 159 pages/40c
WORDSWORTH Edited by David Ferry 160 pages/40c
SEVENTEENTH-CENTURY ENGLISH MINOR POETS 192 pages/35c
Edited by Anne Ferry
EIGHTEENTH-CENTURY ENGLISH MINOR POETS 240 pages/75c
Edited by Mackie L. Jarrell and William Meredith
NINETEENTH-CENTURY BRITISH MINOR POETS 384 pages/75c
Edited by W. H. Auden

Related Books:

POETRY: A Modern Guide to Its Understanding and Enjoyment
by Elizabeth Drew 288 pages/60c
A JOURNEY OF POEMS: An Original Anthology of Verse
Edited by Richard F. Niebling 192 pages/45c
SIX CENTURIES OF GREAT POETRY Edited by Robert Penn
Warren and Albert Erskine 544 pages/95c
VOICES OF POETRY Edited by Allen Kirschner 208 pages/60c

If you cannot obtain copies of these titles from your local bookseller, just send the price (plus 15c per copy for handling and postage) to Dell Books, Post Office Box 1000, Pinebrook, N. J. 07058. No postage or handling charge is required on any order of five or more books.